Where Does God Fit In?

Jim Hockaday

Where Does God Fit In?

P.O. Box 839
Broken Arrow, OK 74013

ISBN: 1-893301-15-X (pbk.)

Original Cover Art:
Interior Design: Cathleen Kwas
Editor: Dr. Larry Keefauver

Acknowledgments

I acknowledge and worship my Father God for His revelation and the grace given to me to humbly produce yet another book. I am always grateful to my family for their love and support, which inspires and encourages the gift of God in me. I am extremely blessed to have many great friendships from an ever-increasing camaraderie of individuals who consider it a privilege to honor God with their bold and daring faith. Remember, He's coming back soon! What an awesome responsibility to be busy about His work.

Table of Contents

INTRODUCTION

Have You Been Wondering?

Ever wonder where God fits in?

Certainly He's around. God's everywhere. But when you need Him, does He often seem distant, detached and hard to reach?

Maybe your bills have been stacking up; car not working; too many trips to the doctor; feeling blah spiritually; having conflict in your relationships; tired of the routine of life?

God never designed the earth to present man with so many distractions. Everything around us seems to say, look at me. The schedule is so hectic that you don't have time to pray, read the Bible or worship. It seems impossible to fit God in. So how do you?

- If God did fit in, would you even recognize His presence?
- Would you be listening for His voice?

- Could you recognize His footprints alongside of yours in the sands of life's journeys?

Is God fitting in simply a mattering of you squeezing Him into a hectic day or a muddled existence?

Ever wonder about these things or is your life so filled with distractions that there's not even time to wonder anymore?

The psalmist said in Psalm 46:10 "Be still, and know that I am God." A simple understanding of this verse is to avoid the trap of letting your attentions be divided and to prioritize your time with God. Obviously, you have picked up this book. You've taken time to ask the question, "Where does God fit in?" Now it's time to step back from life's busyness and into God's presence. He's there. Waiting patiently for you to be all that He's created you to be. Yet, the desire must be burning in you, to change from the commonplace to God's place.

Ready? Let's begin. This journey into God's place will access the wonders of always knowing *where God does fit in!*

CHAPTER 1

So Where Does God Fit In?

Where can I go from Your Spirit?
Or where can I flee from Your presence?

If I ascend into heaven, You are there;
If I make my bed in hell, behold, You are there.

If I take the wings of the morning,
And dwell in the uttermost parts of the sea,

Even there Your hand shall lead me,
And Your right hand shall hold me.

(Psalm 139:7-10)

Can anyone hide from God? As children we often played hide and seek with our parents. For a while, we thought that we had fooled them and they wouldn't find us. But ultimately, we were always found at the end of the game. From the beginning of time in the Garden of Eden, man condemned by sin has tried to hide from

God. However, hiding never works. God is everywhere — omnipresent.

David recognized this truth many millennia ago when he wrote in Psalm 139 that there is no place "where I can flee from Your presence" (verse 7). In this psalm, we see the world's inability to hide from God in some nook or cranny. The truth is revealed: *God's presence is everywhere.*

Since God's presence is everywhere, then why don't we see the evidence? When a deer glides through the fresh fallen snow, we see tracks. When a heavily perfumed lady leaves an elevator, we can still smell her scent. When a person touches a shiny mirror, the evidence of his fingerprint is left behind. Tracking God should be as simple and as real as these examples given.

Seeing the Invisible

We must be equipped to see the invisible. Being born of the Spirit of God provides great access into spiritual things. Seeing that natural man is not in tune with the invisible, most will never easily perceive the supernatural presence of God. Yet it's possible to see the invisible and thus perceive, know and understand "where God fits in."

God is a Spirit and His activity towards man is first spiritual. In every man there is a natural pursuit to understand this spiritual realm for ultimate success. The devil is also a spirit. Remember though, he is a fallen angel who has been defeated by our Lord and Savior. The devil, however, understands the importance of this world's system being in opposition toward faith in God. He uses the natural world and the ignorance of the majority of the earth's population, concerning God's love, as a weapon against God. Obviously not every spirit is of God.

The Apostle John writes,

> *Beloved, do not believe every spirit, but test the spirits, whether they are of God; because many false prophets have gone out into the world. By this you know the Spirit of God: Every spirit that confesses that Jesus Christ has come in the flesh is of God, and every spirit that does not confess that Jesus Christ has come in the flesh is not of God. And this is the spirit of the Antichrist, which you have heard was coming, and is now already in the world.* (1 John 4:1-3)

All around us we see the world yearning for spiritual things. Thus things that are religious and new age have become very trendy and popular. In order to perceive, know, understand and act in faith on "where God fits in," we must be able to "see" the invisible, the Spirit of God at work in the world around us.

Miracles

Miracles happen constantly. However, most people miss the miracles because they are not living in the miraculous, seeing the invisible, staying connected to the supernatural and walking in the Spirit.

Miracles happen constantly. However, most people miss the miracles because they are not living in the miraculous, seeing the invisible, staying connected to the supernatural and walking in the Spirit. If you have not already, I encourage you to read two of my earlier books to develop a deeper understanding of all that I am teaching you in this book. Read *Until I Come* and *Living in the Miraculous.*

Miracles surprise us. Why is that? Let me draw you a picture. In a defensive driving course, we are taught to look for everything happening in our field of vision. We are not simply concentrating on what's in front of us, but we are intentionally aware of everything happening around us — continually glancing in the side and rear view mirrors. When we are focused on defensive driving, we expect the unexpected — new developments that suddenly appear out of nowhere.

Likewise, when we are focused spiritually on what God is doing, we are able to perceive and understand the new, unexpected things that He allows to constantly spring up in our paths. God declares,

Do not remember the former things,
Nor consider the things of old.
Behold, I will do a new thing,
Now it shall spring forth;
Shall you not know it?
I will even make a road in the wilderness
And rivers in the desert.

(Isaiah 43:18-19)

Removing Old Vision

Old perspectives, mindsets and worldly paradigms simply keep us from seeing *where God fits in.* Perhaps you wore glasses as a child and now twenty years later you tried to wear those same glasses. What once was clear is now blurred. The old prescription for seeing simply doesn't work for today. No longer does the past bring any clarity or vision to the present. You need a new prescription for seeing.

The same is true with God. Old ways of doing and saying things, old habits that bind up and constrict us, must be discarded. Instead, God's vision and perspective must be grasped in order to see what God is doing. We need to see through His eyes in order to recognize His activity in the world around us.

Vision

OLD WAYS OF DOING AND SAYING THINGS, OLD HABITS THAT BIND UP AND CONSTRICT US, MUST BE DISCARDED. INSTEAD, GOD'S VISION AND PERSPECTIVE MUST BE GRASPED IN ORDER TO SEE WHAT GOD IS DOING.

The vision that the world gives is cursed. It is clouded by fear, greed, intimidation and self. James writes, "For where you have envy and selfish ambition, there you find disorder and every evil practice" (James 3:16 NIV). No wonder so many works of the devil are manifest. It has been ingrained in us since birth to see things and think about them from the world's perspective. If we think like the world, then we will be good at revealing the world. I am thankful that God has higher ways and thoughts than we do.

God's Word has good news for the bad report we have in the world. God's power exists for us to be set free from the old things of the past and to be healed. Luke records a wonderful story, a good report, in Luke 5:17, "One day as he [Jesus] was teaching, Pharisees and teachers of the law, who had come from every village of Galilee and from Judea and Jerusalem, were sitting there. And the power of the Lord was present for him to heal the sick" (NIV).

Notice that the power was there with Jesus but the Pharisees and teachers of the law were blind to it. How so? Jesus revealed that the hearts of the Pharisees and teachers of the law where so hard, and their motives where so evil, that they were of their father the devil. Their desire to accuse and judge Jesus was too important for these men to sense the presence of the Lord. They were blind to the good news that Jesus, God's Son, was right there with them. Jesus was there to save, heal and deliver them from the old. Something new, miraculous and wonderful would happen in their lives if they could only see it!

A heart hardened by the world's perspective will alienate a person from God. The Apostle Paul warns us, "You should no longer walk as the rest of the Gentiles walk, in the futility of their mind, having their understanding darkened, being alienated from the life of God, because of the ignorance that is in them, because of the blindness of their heart; who, being past feeling, have given themselves over to lewdness, to work all uncleanness with greediness" (Ephesians 4:17-19).

Now that Jesus has been raised from the dead, God's

power and life through the risen Christ is always present to heal. When Jesus is present, His power is on the scene. The Scripture declares that the power of the Lord was present to heal the sick. There is no indication that only one would be healed. On the contrary, you would assume that there would be more than one sick person for the power was present to heal them.

This brings up a very interesting question. Could God be present and people not even know it? Let's go even further. Could God be present and preachers not know it? Is Jesus present by His Spirit in and around us? If we trust Him as Lord and Savior, He has promised to be with us always, even to the end of the age. Whenever two or more meet together in His name, Jesus is there. Do we have the vision to see His presence and trust His healing power?

God's Presence
Whenever two or more meet together in His name, Jesus is there. Do we have the vision to see His presence and trust His healing power?

Or, if we look, see and perceive each day as it appears, with its own dictates of what will be, then we are at the mercy of the circumstances that come our way. If there is nothing we can do about disaster, then fate decides whether or not we are its victims.

God has a great desire to pick up the slack for us, make the difference and more than overwhelmingly supply us with ability to last a lifetime.

Yet the decision rests with you and me. Are we willing to let go of the past? Will the Lord, who is present today in our lives to bless us, be given the freedom to do in us and through us what He desires? Can we truly see the invisible and do the impossible?

As born again, new creations in Christ, who have been set free from all old things and placed into the new things of God, we have the ability to see the "invisible." We can be naturally supernatural in all we see, say and do. Let's discover together how that happens so that we can know *how God fits in* to each day, each circumstance, each conversation, each action, and every thought or feeling.

CHAPTER 2

Naturally Supernatural

Let me show you just how natural the supernatural is. Remember that you can do away with the old, natural and habitual ways of doing and seeing things. You can be naturally supernatural. Elijah and Elisha discovered this reality. So can you.

In 2 Kings 2:8, we read of how Elijah began in the natural to live supernaturally, "Now Elijah took his mantle, rolled it up, and struck the water; and it was divided this way and that, so that the two of them crossed over on dry ground."

The mantle that Elijah rolled up and used to strike the water was powerfully anointed with the Spirit of God. Certainly he must have felt this power like electricity. So, how could he hold all that power in his hand?

Elisha was a companion of Elijah. He asked Elijah for a double portion of the anointing that was on his life.

Elijah told Elisha that if he saw him being taken up into heaven, then the anointing would be as he asked.

> *And Elisha saw it, and he cried out, "My father, my father, the chariot of Israel and its horsemen!" So he saw him no more. And he took hold of his own clothes and tore them into two pieces. He also took up the mantle of Elijah that had fallen from him, and went back and stood by the bank of the Jordan. Then he took the mantle of Elijah that had fallen from him, and struck the water, and said, "Where is the LORD God of Elijah?" And when he also had struck the water, it was divided this way and that; and Elisha crossed over.*
>
> 2 Kings 2:12-14)

These verses show us that indeed Elisha was present when Elijah was taken up. The mantle that had fallen to the ground represented the double portion of anointing. Surely Elisha would sense or feel the presence of God. At least you would think so, right?

Notice, he took the mantle and had to ask, "Where is the LORD God of Elijah?" At the same time, he struck the water as Elijah did in verse 8. All of this indicates so much. Elisha couldn't feel the anointing. Nothing in the natural realm indicated that Elijah had left anything for Elisha.

Elisha functioned in the natural until he did what his predecessor had done to prove whether or not he possessed the power of Elijah. Obviously we would say, don't start a ministry, and don't move in the miraculous or declare the impossible, if God isn't in it.

If God is In It, Act!

As we can see from verse 14, the water divided exactly as it did for Elijah. Elisha walked over on dry ground as they had done previously. This experiment was crucial for Elisha. It would prove whether or not God would be with Elisha as He had been with Elijah. If Elisha was to believe for twice the results, then he had to know that God's power was present in His life and that he was comfortable using it to do miraculous works.

Even though Elisha felt nothing in the natural, he was willing to take a risk to move in the supernatural. While he could not "feel" the power of God naturally, he took the leap of faith to see God move supernaturally.

A Leap of Faith

EVEN THOUGH ELISHA FELT NOTHING IN THE NATURAL, HE WAS WILLING TO TAKE A RISK TO MOVE IN THE SUPERNATURAL. WHILE HE COULD NOT "FEEL" THE POWER OF GOD NATURALLY, HE TOOK THE LEAP OF FAITH TO SEE GOD MOVE SUPERNATURALLY.

There are times when you can sense God's power working within you. Of course, if God allowed these mortal bodies of ours to feel the fullness of His power, we probably couldn't handle it. The point that I would like you to understand is that Elisha began his ministry trusting in the power that he couldn't detect physically. So actually, working the miraculous for this Old Testament prophet was very natural to the senses, yet supernatural in its effect. Elisha moved naturally in the supernatural.

This does not exclude the power of God from being sensed in a very tangible way. As Luke 5 mentions, the power of the Lord was present or sensed naturally. The undeniable fact that can stand on its own merit is this: *Your time in the Word will reveal God's intentions and directions, and your time in His presence will endear your heart to the ultimate will of God for your life.*

A man or woman who understands his or her God-given rights and privileges while having spent time with the Bible's Author will be undefeated. The problems of the world will never surpass the God-kind of help and guidance. So then, where does God fit in?

Anywhere you let Him.

The Promise of Resting in Him

> *Therefore, since the promise of entering his rest still stands, let us be careful that none of you be found to have fallen short of it. For we also have had the gospel preached to us, just as they did; but the message they heard was of no value to them, because those who heard did not combine it with faith. Now we who have believed enter that rest, just as God has said,*
> *"So I declared an oath in my anger,*
> *'They shall never enter my rest.'"*
>
> *And yet his work has been finished since the creation of the world.*
>
> (Hebrews 4:1-3 NIV)

When God speaks and His power is made known, some will listen and some will not. As with the children of Israel, there was a whole generation who needlessly died out because of their unbelief. Ten times they tested God until they reaped exactly what they sowed. God's intention wasn't that they should die in the wilderness. He was ready to take them into the promised land to inherit all that He promised them. In fact, as the third verse says, the works were already finished before the foundation of the world. The works represent the success and joy of living in the promised land flowing with milk and honey. Their rebellion and stubbornness was the cause of their failure.

Listen

In such a time as we are living, it pays to listen to God.
God never fits into our lives without our willingness to hear and obey Him.

In such a time as we are living, it pays to listen to God. God never fits into our lives without our willingness to hear and obey him.

Many have questioned the recent events in our nation. Where was God on 9/11? First of all, Jesus never said there wouldn't be trials in the world. He did say, however, that we were not to fear, for he had overcome all tribulation. God's grace and mercy are always active.

We are blessed to have God's assistance available to us at all times. Jesus promised to be with us always even until the end of time.

And Jesus came and spoke to them, saying, "All authority has been given to Me in heaven and on earth. Go therefore and make disciples of all the nations, baptizing them in the name of the Father and of the Son and of the Holy Spirit, teaching them to observe all things that I have commanded you; and lo, I am with you always, even to the end of the age." Amen. (Matthew 28:18-20).

GOD AT WORK
GOD IS ALWAYS WORKING BEHIND THE SCENES, BIRTHING POSSIBILITIES AND POSITIONING US FOR SUCCESS.

God is always working behind the scenes, birthing possibilities and positioning us for success. It's up to us to be constantly vigilant and watching for where God is at work and then join Him in doing what He is doing!

When we heed the directions of the Lord, disaster is averted and failure is bypassed. Many thousands of people avoided the disaster of 9/11. They were either consciously or subconsciously led not to be in that area at that time, or they were delayed in some way.

The evil that is in the world is directly or indirectly inspired by the devil. Satan hates God and desires nothing less than to annihilate anything that resembles Him. Even the war fought over the land of Israel is much more complex than who says they have rights. God gave the land to His chosen people, Israel. End of story! The devil wants more than to take some land away from God's chosen people. He wants to annihilate the race of Jews. No matter what it looks like, the enemy will not succeed. Many dangerous things happen to people because either one or many have not heeded the direction of the Lord.

When looking at the problems of life, we must properly interpret what method of escape should apply. "No temptation has overtaken you except such as is common to man; but God is faithful, who will not allow you to be tempted beyond what you are able, but with the temptation will also make the way of escape, that you may be able to bear it" (1 Corinthians 10:13).

In His goodness, God provides avenues of victory. Every temptation and danger can be faced and victory manifested when God is in our thoughts and actions. However, we must define the problems of life. On one hand there is the deliverance and victory found in redemption over the effects of sin in your own life. In all of these, God makes a way of escape. On the other hand, because of sin, there are wages to pay. Spiritual death is the greatest penalty.

Man was born into sin, and will continue to reap the wages of sin unless he becomes born again. The wages of sin include sickness and disease, poverty, habits and addictions. All the works of darkness that man was held in bondage to are released through the new birth. We become recipients or containers of the divine nature of God. This divine nature is the power of God that frees us to walk in liberty over all the works of darkness.

We will get to some other classifications of problems after first looking at how we can overcome the curses of sin. To start with, every curse of sin is under the blood of Jesus. What He accomplished in His death, burial and resurrection was ultimately for our release.

Overcoming the Curse of Spiritual Death

Sin

Jesus' death on the cross and the bearing of our sins upon Himself releases all humanity from the dreary outlook of sin.

The most important area of an individual's life is whether or not that person has been liberated from the bondage of spiritual death. Paul said that all have sinned and fallen short of the glory of God (Romans 2:23). Because no one can become righteous alone, there is a great need in the heart of man. Jesus came first and foremost to abolish the separation between God and man.

Jesus' death on the cross and the bearing of our sins upon Himself releases all humanity from the dreary outlook of sin. Jesus identified Himself with us so that we could accept by faith the new identity of His salvation. The fact that so many reject the privilege of eternal salvation doesn't mean that it isn't provided for all. John 1 affirms that as many as receive Him, to them He gave the power to become sons of God (John 1:12).

Scripture declares that whosoever calls upon the name of the Lord, shall be saved (Romans 10:13). This simple definition of the need for salvation should make very clear the understanding of our responsibility to preach the gospel. If someone will share the good news that Jesus has provided a way to eternal life, at least calculated decisions can be made.

Romans 10:14-17 tells us that when a preacher preaches, people hear. When you hear correctly, you can believe correctly. If you believe, you will call on the name of the Lord and be saved. God desperately wants you to be saved. However, you alone are the only one who can receive it. No one can call on the name of Jesus for you. You must make that decision yourself.

Let's answer the simple question, "Where does God fit in with the salvation of the world?"

God solved the problem of sin when He sent Jesus to the earth. Jesus is the Messiah, the Savior of the world. When Jesus died, God was in Christ, meaning that He was working through the death, burial and resurrection to accomplish what no one else could do; namely, save the entire world.

Salvation

THE WORLD NEEDS TO KNOW THAT THE DEBT OF SIN HAS BEEN CANCELLED AND SALVATION IS OFFERED TO ALL WHO CALL UPON THE NAME OF THE LORD.

Jesus carried the sin for all time — past, present and future, when He went to the grave. He buried our sin and was raised up for the entire world as a champion over spiritual death. The world needs to know that the debt of sin has been cancelled and salvation is offered to all who call upon the name of the Lord. And yet, only those who know and call upon the name of the Lord will secure for themselves this great privilege.

Once saved, as believers we have the power and privilege to overcome all of life's negative situations. Knowing that you possess the supernatural answer to life's problems will, as Elisha discovered, release you to live in that realm.

In the next chapter, we will discover some of the ways "that God fits in" as we look specifically at obstacles like sin and sickness, lack, bondage, and problems in marriage and relationships.

CHAPTER 3

Overcoming Life's Negatives

Life is filled with attacks. Some attacks come from enemies, others from friends or circumstances.

- So, where does God fit in when negatives attack us from circumstances and relationships?
- How do we overcome through His Word and trusting in His ways?

Where Does God Fit In When We're Sick?

God doesn't make faulty creations. When He made man, there was no sickness and disease. The effect of sin was twofold. Genesis 2:17 reveals to us that when man sinned, he would die twice. The first death was spiritual death — separation from God. The second death was the death of the physical body.

Sickness

Healing, as a part of the Old Covenant, meant that sickness was never allowed if God's people would honor Him and reverence His Word.

It makes sense that if the

physical body came alive when God breathed into the nostrils of Adam, then it would die if spiritual death became the ruler of the heart. John Alexander Dowie said that sickness and disease are the foul offspring of their father Satan and their mother sin.

Man's desperate need for healing would be met by a covenant from God, whereby He would pledge His services forever as the great physician. Healing, as a part of the old covenant, meant that sickness was never allowed if God's people would honor Him and reverence His Word.

God spoke to Moses declaring that He would not allow His people to get sick if they would obey Him, for He was the God that healed them:

> *"If you diligently heed the voice of the LORD your God and do what is right in His sight, give ear to His commandments and keep all His statutes, I will put none of the diseases on you which I have brought on the Egyptians: For I am the LORD who heals you"* (Exodus 15:26).

Consider God's definition of healing: *never getting sick.* If God really were your Healer, then His power of healing would eliminate sickness before it could take hold of you. Enough healing abided in God's covenant with Israel to keep multitudes of Israelites in the wilderness well and healthy.

However, their covenant, enforced by the blood of bulls and goats to meet the conditions for sacrifice, is an inferior covenant to the one we possess in Christ Jesus. "Jesus has become a surety of a better covenant" (Hebrews 7:22).

Today, our covenant is sealed by the blood of the Lord Jesus Christ. Christ insures, becomes the guarantee and surety, of, the new covenant. Never again will sickness be a great difficulty for the Christian. However, as long as the world and the church allow sickness a place, there will be a need for healing.

God's provision conquers problems caused by sin. As you can see, God's provision for any difficulty that man will ever face is far greater than the problems of sin. Sickness and disease has become an accepted evil in the world. Christian and sinner alike fear the clutches of sickness and disease. To most, even in the body of Christ, the doctor has replaced God.

The church needs a revival of divine healing. A restoration is necessary for the church to recognize its failure and return to the strength of divine healing. The world is ripe for the church to rise up and produce the works of Jesus.

Sickness

DIVINE HEALING WILL WORK FOR THOSE WHO KNOW GOD AND THOSE WHO DON'T.

So *where does God fit in* concerning divine healing? God so loves the world that He desires to bless us all every way He can. When we consider the riches of God's mercy, we see Him heal all who will allow Him to. God is not partial to those who are in covenant. Divine healing will work for those who know God and those who don't. When someone doesn't comprehend the love of God to heal, we are thankful for the wisdom He gives to the medical profession. Medical science has captivated the conscience of nearly all men. We are thankful for the many who are helped and whose lives are preserved. However, the return to the knowledge of divine healing and its application is a must in our modern day. The truth of divine healing must permeate the world and produce among men the highest hope for ultimate success over all sickness and disease.

Isn't it God's mercy to keep someone well long enough to hear the gospel message and receive Jesus as Lord and Healer? If so, then they will have the privilege of walking in divine health with Jesus as their Great Physician. To the Christian, God is right where He belongs, living inside of us. We are the temple of the living God, the place where God dwells in the earth.

Christ has defeated the devil and all sickness and all disease as a significant part of our redemption. What Jesus did in respect to healing is available today, just as our salvation is available now.

SICKNESS
WHAT JESUS DID 2000 YEARS AGO WORKS *TODAY* FOR YOU. YOUR **FAITH** IN HIM WILL SECURE THE BLESSING OF DIVINE HEALTH.

In the Greek, the word for salvation, *sozo,* also means healing and wholeness. The full work of salvation is available to all who trust Jesus. If church history records divine healing for the past 2000 years as a valid form of ministry, then it's obvious that God hasn't left His post. What Jesus did 2000 years ago works today for you. Your faith in Him will secure the blessing of divine health.

Faith will always work when rooted in God's Word. If the Word of God gives us reason to believe that God desires His children to be healed, then this blessing can be appropriated through faith. The law of faith works by an action empowered by trusting God's Word to release that desired blessing in God. Faith in God that's rooted in His Word releases the supernatural into the natural, the invisible into the visible and the will of God on earth as it is in heaven. Once released, God's blessing of healing must be accepted or received in order for healing to be manifested.

Let me give you an example. Someone gives you a check for $100. A check isn't cash. The signature on the check verifies the funds to be paid. Similarly, the Word of God for healing is signed and sealed, verified and guaranteed, by the shed blood of Christ. *By His stripes we are healed.* Now to take that check to the bank to be cashed is an act of faith. No cash can be received until the promise represented in that check is acted upon.

Almost seventy-five years ago, a noted healing evangelist named Smith Wigglesworth often preached a simple message for those desiring healing. He declared this simple truth: *faith acts!*

Once the check is cashed and money is received, a final appropriation must be made. The cash doesn't accomplish anything until it's spent. Whatever is bought with that cash is the manifestation. When faith is "spent" or appropriated — used in the natural, then healing is manifested.

The human body works by the design of God. The most natural force and substance that a human body can receive and transmit is the power of God. Every cell can be surcharged by the life of God until healing overpowers any and all sickness. This action is not just divine healing, but divine health.

Please understand that as simple as all this sounds on paper, divine healing was made to be even easier in practice. The consciousness of modern Christianity has all but destroyed the ease of redemption to meet the need of the world. As sad as this sounds, it's even worse when you consider the magnitude of the ship of unbelief that must be quickly turned.

Let me ask:

Sickness

If you need healing, why not trust in the supply of God's healing power and receive your healing now?

- If you need healing, why not trust in the supply of God's healing power and receive your healing now?
- Why not believe in the power of God to arrest the sickness and eradicate the disease from your body?

- Why not let divine healing once again challenge the doctrines of the world with demonstrations that can be verified?
- Why not cash and spend the check you have in your hand? In other words; hear, believe, and act in faith!

Jesus is your Great Physician; this truth will never change. When sick, let God fit into your life by expelling the illness and breathing life into your body and soul by His indwelling Spirit.

Where Does God Fit Into Lack or Poverty?

The Apostle John writes, "Beloved, I pray that you may prosper in all things and be in health, just as your soul prospers" (3 John 2).

The issue of lack or poverty has already been decided on or settled long ago by Jesus as a surety of the new covenant. Prosperity has always been to God as a hand in a glove. You cannot find God anywhere without an over abundance of whatever is needed. He is *El Shaddai,* the God who sees before the need and makes provision in abundance. Some call Him "the God of more than enough."

Prosperity, as the Apostle John declares, should be a part of our whole life. The sum total of God, which cannot be measured, makes life extremely full. Prosperity should be in all things, including health. Our soul is the first necessary ingredient of prosperity that will support the full plan of God.

What you traditionally understand about the subject of prosperity can greatly hinder you from receiving your blessings. If money to you were an evil, then you would want to avoid it altogether. As you can see, this would be a foolish argument. Money is not evil, however the love of money is. You could be rich or poor and covet money.

Most people cannot handle wealth. They would lose it without having used it wisely.

Money was made to bless and then be a blessing. The greatest joy of life is in giving. God loved the world and gave. When the perspective of the heart is changed, then money becomes a vehicle for the overall good of God's plan on the earth. Let me ask you:

- How many people do you know who are debt free?
- How many churches do people attend that are run down, and in need of repair?
- How many churches carry a great debt?
- How many Christians are looking for a handout, instead of seeking to hand something out?
- How many people do you hear regularly complain about those who have money?
- How many people do you know who grumble constantly about where they are financially, instead of developing their minds in the Word concerning prosperity?
- How many people can't enjoy doing things in life because they don't have the money?

- Would you agree with me that the church has a money problem? Where is God in all of this?

In John 6:4-6 Jesus teaches us a great lesson, "Now the Passover, a feast of the Jews, was near. Then Jesus lifted up His eyes, and seeing a great multitude coming toward Him, He said to Philip, 'Where shall we buy bread, that these may eat?' But this He said to test him, for He Himself knew what He would do."

I like the phrase: *for He Himself knew what He would do.* This shows me that Jesus recognized the supply of increase that God had made available for blessing. Increase is something that God continually does for His children. Within God's Spirit flows a continual anointing to prosper, a supply of wealth that you must receive and release by faith in order to personally prosper.

In Mark 6:37, we read a story about the crowds following Jesus and being hungry. Jesus told the disciples to feed the crowd. His disciples were focusing on what they saw in the natural instead of what Jesus knew supernaturally. So they asked, "Shall we go and buy two hundred denarii's worth of bread and give them something to eat?"

Lack & Poverty
Within God's Spirit flows a continual anointing to prosper, a supply of wealth that you must receive and release by faith in order to personally prosper.

Consider this: Jesus wasn't asking His disciples to do something that couldn't be done. He commanded his disciples to work a miracle because it was possible. Jesus knew what could be done naturally through the supernatural power of God's ever-present power and grace. Jesus knew the supernatural laws that govern God's economy.

Recognizing the supply of increase that governs financial growth is what makes possible your miracle. The disciples could have actually worked the miracle that Jesus worked if they had known what to do. There are definitely areas in your life that God has made available as avenues for financial increase. What you do with them will determine your growth.

Following the laws of sowing and reaping, and listening to the voice of the Lord will definitely change your finances. Let me ask you:

- How has your giving been lately? What is the condition of your sowing?
- What about the tithe?
- What about the giving of offerings?
- What about your attitude toward your job?
- Have you been diligently working, or just getting by?

God specifically says that what we sow and the manner in which we sow determines how it shall come back to us.

Would God receive any glory in your poverty? As parents, does it make us happy when our children go without? God cares about us and has made provision for us all to walk in wealth. The application begins with our acceptance of God's supernatural law of sowing and reaping. We apply the law by faith, by acting upon it.

Let me help you understand something very vital. What people believe is what they *act upon* by faith. Faith is more than what you confess. You may confess one thing and act on another. What you act on is what you really believe. Lack is defeated as you give cheerfully and rejoice by faith in God's prosperity.

Lack & Poverty
LACK IS DEFEATED AS YOU GIVE CHEERFULLY AND REJOICE BY FAITH IN GOD'S PROSPERITY.

To hold onto stuff and be tight fisted is to walk in a poverty mentality. God desires that we look beyond our present circumstances and begin to give and to rejoice about what we believe we have received.

- Is prosperity something that we will have someday or can we experience it right now?
- Aren't all of God's benefits received in the heart before they become visible?
- How about you? Are you a rich person? Are all of your needs met? Will you ever have a money problem?

Where Does God Fit In When We Walk in Bondage?

Now the Lord is the Spirit, and where the Spirit of the Lord is, there is freedom. (2 Corinthians 3:17 NIV)

Thank God, the Spirit of the Lord is living in us. The indwelling Holy Spirit brings freedom into every situation and relationship that would seek to bind us. Freedom is built into the very DNA of our spirits.

Redemption will get you excited this way. Everything that is necessary to live and to function in life is a by-product of our salvation. If the Holy Ghost lives in us, then there is a liberty for all things to be remedied. It's not necessary that we look elsewhere for our liberty.

We don't need to look to others, or to society, or to government to free us. When everything is in bondage around us, we are free on the inside. Jesus made an astounding statement in Luke chapter five when He said to the paralytic man, "Son, your sins are forgiven you." Believing that Jesus had the power and authority to forgive sins may not surprise us, except that this act meant that complete restoration was also in the package. Luke 5:20-26 reads,

> *When He saw their faith, He said to him, "Man, your sins are forgiven you." And the scribes and the Pharisees began to reason, saying, "Who is this who speaks blasphemies? Who can forgive sins but God alone?"*
>
> *But when Jesus perceived their thoughts, He answered and said to them, "Why are you reasoning in your hearts? Which is easier, to say, 'Your sins are forgiven you,' or to say, 'Rise up and walk'? But that you may know that the Son of Man has power on earth to forgive sins" — He said to the man who was paralyzed, "I say to you, arise, take up your bed, and go to your house."*

Immediately he rose up before them, took up what he had been lying on, and departed to his own house, glorifying God.

Look closely at Jesus' statement in verse 23, ". . . which is easier, to say, 'Your sins are forgiven you,' or to say, 'Rise up and walk?'" To the Jewish mind and understanding of covenant, the moment you are free from sin, you gain every available portion of benefit. The Jews only knew themselves to have difficulty with sickness and the wicked results of the curse if they had missed God. The lack of protection would also fall in this category. Once a relationship was restored with God, it was common knowledge to expect restoration.

When Jesus said your sins are forgiven, it was the same as saying that your restoration is complete. The man could have walked right then, if he had acted. This is why so much of the Apostle Paul's writings failed to include healing messages like we have interpreted today. We don't find complete healing sermons to the early church, as we might have imagined. Paul, being a devout Jew, understood that when we are born again and come into complete righteousness, at that very moment, sickness fails to be an issue.

Redemption is not just forgiveness of sins, as we have believed it to be. Forgiveness of sins according to Paul means that we walk in divine health and freedom. Redemption releases the full gospel — the total work of the cross in every area of our lives.

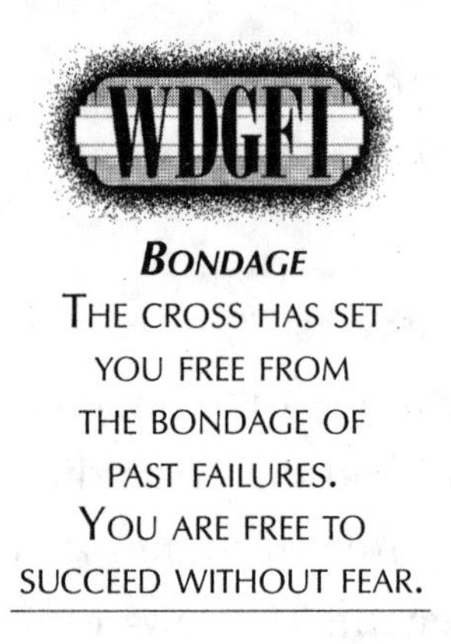

The cross has set you free from the bondage of past failures. You are free to succeed without fear. Your past has no power over your present or future. Your bondage from the past doesn't determine your future, God does! By faith, your destiny is now in His hands!

If we had understood this from our new birth experience we would have avoided many serious difficulties. Most Christians have learned that salvation is easy, however, everything else in life is very frustrating and difficult.

Jesus was very specific about the anointing that was upon Him. Luke 4:18-19, "The Spirit of the Lord is upon me, because he anointed me to preach the gospel to the poor. He has sent me to proclaim release to the captives, and recovery of sight to the blind, to set free those who are oppressed, to proclaim the favorable year of the Lord." (NASU)

Jesus said that the anointing would release all captives and set free those who are oppressed. The salvation message is such good news! The moment we are saved, we should be loosed from any bondage. Walking around with all the same problems outwardly is not acceptable to the work of our Lord. God has supplied us with grace that will conquer any past violation of purity. To remain bound really means that we are not willing to yield to the Spirit's strength and ability within us.

So, if you feel guilty, you have a choice. The truth is, you're forgiven! If you encounter any bondage in your life that you can't shake, begin yielding to the power of redemption. The truth is, you're free! If you walk in sickness, then choose by faith to walk in health. The truth is, you're healed!

You will remain in bondage as long as you prefer ignorance to knowing by faith the living Christ who has set you free! Jesus says to you, "And you shall know the truth, and the truth shall make you free" (John 8:32). You are a new creation, a new person in Christ (2 Corinthians 5:17). Knowing the truth sets you *free* to be all God in Christ has created you to be!

Bondage

YOU WILL REMAIN IN BONDAGE AS LONG AS YOU PREFER IGNORANCE TO KNOWING BY FAITH THE LIVING CHRIST WHO HAS SET YOU FREE!

Why do we experience bondage?

Usually it's the result of ignorance concerning our liberty in Christ. You will find that the devil will always coerce people away from their consciousness of victory. The area of bondage where most people struggle is a weakness in their thoughts. Is the power there? Is God's victory real? Yes it is, however, changing one's perception is in the hands of the believer.

Where Does God Fit In When Relationships Are Hurtful?

Let's examine other problems that exist beyond the curses that accompany sin. These problems have to do with our relationships.

Marriage. Oh that all things concerning marriage were simple. As soon as other people are involved, there is a need for maturity. Sin, the world and the devil's system have all taught us how to yield to the flesh without thinking. We habitually respond to life's struggles based on our past training or experiences.

If we choose to live life without making our minds submit to the Word of God, we will hopelessly live out of complete selfishness. Life would become a survival of the fittest. God desires that every area of our lives be affected by redemption.

The greatest institution outside of our relationship with the Lord Jesus is marriage. If God instituted this union, then He must have provided it with the ability to succeed. Anything less than marital oneness is unacceptable to the Lord. Just as in every other area of redemption, our experience with the will of the Lord is a matter of walking in the light of the Word by faith. As much as the emphasis for success incorporates faith, we should be excited instead of frustrated with God's methods.

What a privilege it is to honor God's Word, by accepting and trusting God's ways to work. The easiest thing a believer can do is to believe. Every work of the Lord from

His perspective is the easiest thing He could require of us. Maturing beyond the flesh and learning to develop a spirit consciousness should become our goal for life.

Paul gives us some great insight concerning the responsibilities in marriage.

> *Wives, submit to your husbands as to the Lord. For the husband is the head of the wife as Christ is the head of the church, his body, of which he is the Savior. Now as the church submits to Christ, so also wives should submit to their husbands in everything.*
>
> *Husbands, love your wives, just as Christ loved the church and gave himself up for her to make her holy, cleansing her by the washing with water through the word, and to present her to himself as a radiant church, without stain or wrinkle or any other blemish, but holy and blameless.*
>
> *In this same way, husbands ought to love their wives as their own bodies. He who loves his wife loves himself. After all, no one ever hated his own body, but he feeds and cares for it, just as Christ does the church – for we are members of his body. "For this reason a man will leave his father and mother and be united to his wife, and the two will become one flesh." This is a profound mystery –but I am talking about Christ and the church. However, each one of you also must love his wife as he loves himself, and the wife must respect her husband.*
>
> (Ephesians 5:22-23 NIV)

As we can see, there are specific responsibilities designed for each partner in the marriage union. *Responsibility is the key ingredient for success.* God gives husbands responsibility for loving their wives as Christ loves the church; He gives wives responsibility to submit to their husbands.

When hurting marriages break in separation or divorce, one or both mates refuse to take responsibility for both the problems and the faith needed to seek help and to make changes. Instead of praying, "God change my spouse," both need to take responsibility in praying, "God change me!"

I understand these to be strong and unpopular statements, yet the Lord has distributed assignments to each partner. Where the Lord fits into the relationship, between the husband and the wife, is when each partner participates in the responsibilities given to them. The scriptural thought to the wife is that she come under the authority of, and adapt to her husband. Her love is seen through her willingness to please her husband. This respect for a husband's leadership, and likewise honoring God's command, has nothing to do with whether or not he is doing his part.

HURTING RELATIONSHIPS

RESPONSIBILITY IS THE KEY INGREDIENT FOR SUCCESS. GOD GIVES HUSBANDS *RESPONSIBILITY* FOR LOVING THEIR WIVES AS CHRIST LOVES THE CHURCH; HE GIVES WIVES *RESPONSIBILITY* TO SUBMIT TO THEIR HUSBANDS.

There is much to say to the husband to explain his responsibility. He is to love his wife as Christ loves the church. This love is an unceasing devotion to care for, understand and know the things that would bless his wife. Much sacrifice is necessary to lead and protect his wife and family. By conveying to his wife his devotion and time, he will endear her heart to him.

Again, whether or not the wife is functioning in her place, as she ought, is not the requirement for his accepted responsibility. If God has placed the assignment on the husband to love his wife as Christ loves the church, and as he loves himself, then there is no need to argue over his role of leadership.

The most effective working of the marriage union is where both partners are fulfilling their God given assignments. Looking elsewhere instead of within will never supply your partner with the anointing that God has given to each marriage. God fits very well in every marriage, if the marriage partners will only provide Him with their obedience to His designed strategy for a successful marriage.

Family, Co-Workers and Friends. The answer to a thousand questions, when concerned with others, is, God's love, "Now hope does not disappoint, because the love of God has been poured out in our hearts by the Holy Spirit who was given to us" (Romans 5:5). Only God's unconditional love *(agape)* can give us the power in our hurting relationships to bring forgiveness, healing and reconciliation to one another.

Hurting Relationships
Only God's unconditional love (agape) can give us the power in our hurting relationships to bring forgiveness, healing and reconciliation to one another.

God has made a rich deposit in our hearts of His love that prevails in all situations. We already understand quite well that people are either up or down, happy or sad. One thing we can't count on is what others will do. We certainly must learn not to put our trust ultimately in people. If we fail ourselves, then we are prone to fail others. Thank God for His insight and supply of love as these passages reveal:

> *Therefore, as the elect of God, holy and beloved, put on tender mercies, kindness, humility, meekness, longsuffering; bearing with one another, and forgiving one another, if anyone has a complaint against another; even as Christ forgave you, so you also must do. But above all these things put on love, which is the bond of perfection.* (Colossians 3:12-14)
>
> *And above all things have fervent love for one another, for "love will cover a multitude of sins."* (1 Peter 4:8)

Love is always interested in looking out for the interests of others. To prefer others above self is one of the greatest ways to experience the heart of our Father God. Jesus came as a servant, we can do no less. Since the flesh is selfish and the heart surrendered to Jesus is love, there will be a fight for ownership.

We must battle the flesh with a renewed mind. God is very willing to be involved in our relationships. A steady diet of the Word is the only successful way of acting in love, which ensures God's involvement.

Natural Disasters and Crises

Make no mistake; every natural disaster is orchestrated either directly by the devil or indirectly by the devil working through human evil. God made the earth function perfectly when He created it. When sin entered into the earth, all of creation felt its effect. Now after all these years, the earth needs the salvation of God just as badly as man. It is a sign of the times that the earth is struggling for survival. Now more than ever, more earthquakes, hurricanes, tornados, cyclones, volcanoes and climatic variations are recorded.

Disasters & Crises

MAKE NO MISTAKE; EVERY NATURAL DISASTER IS ORCHESTRATED EITHER DIRECTLY BY THE DEVIL OR INDIRECTLY BY THE DEVIL WORKING THROUGH HUMAN EVIL.

In the book of Job there were natural disasters that killed his sons and daughters. As much as man wants to blame God, it is clearly understood in this book, by looking at the beginning chapter, that Satan was behind this calamity. Job said, "the Lord giveth and the Lord taketh away" (Job 1:21). You may say that God allowed it and that would be true. However, don't make this a negative, but understand that God has to allow many things that He wishes He could avoid.

Looking at the ministry of Jesus we can locate answers to our questions about natural disaster and terrorism. What can we expect? First of all, **the crises of life will come to everyone.** Jesus told His disciples that trials would come, but be of good cheer, for I, meaning Jesus, have overcome them (John 16:33).

Since they have been overcome, then there is hope for us when we are confronted with them. When Jesus dealt with natural disaster He always confronted it. If you will remember, God delegated authority over the earth to Adam. Jesus came as the second Adam to correct the problems caused by sin.

God never made the earth to destroy itself. When God said in Genesis 1:31 that everything He made was very good, do you think natural disasters were accounted for? Of course not! God is not the destroyer. David said in Psalm 103:5 that God has redeemed us from destruction. At destruction and famine — God laughs. Not because it's funny, but because it will never overcome His goodness to counteract it.

When a storm arose on the sea, Jesus rebuked it and commanded peace to replace it. Immediately it became quite and peaceful. Everything in creation serves His purposes. Even the wild beasts refrained from harming Jesus when He was in the wilderness for 40 days before

His temptation by the devil. This is the standard for all who are in Christ. God's ability is always equal to the standard.

In the ministry of the Apostle Paul, he was also confronted with a storm. Before setting sail for Rome, Paul sensed that the voyage would end in disaster. Who was it that gave Paul this premonition? It was the Holy Ghost. Paul knew well enough about following these subtle promptings that he vocalized it to the Centurion. But this godless man sided with the helmsman rather than Paul, who said that the voyage would be fine. They even received a south wind, which spoke of a successful journey.

Just as God knew it would happen, a great storm arose which left the crew frantically fighting for their lives. When all was done naturally to bring security and yet none was to be found, they gave up hope. Then Paul had a vision from God, and an angel appeared to him. The message was clear that the ship would be lost, yet none of the lives of the crew would be harmed. The event happened just as Paul was told.

In this illustration, God was trying to keep Paul and the crew out of danger. Paul obviously went through some disaster on account of the decisions of others. This is a good reason why we should be praying for our president and leaders of other countries. They don't have to be born again to do the will of God. Our prayers will avail much if we will be persistent. Many things happen to people that could be avoided if leaders would make the right decisions.

Disasters & Crises
The direction of the Lord is always timely and for our ultimate good. God is at work in all things for those who love Him and are called according to His purpose (Rom. 8:28 NIV).

Notice that God made provision for Paul's safety and those who were involved with him. In Paul's ministry there were times when the Holy Ghost forbade him to go to certain places. The direction of the Lord is always timely and for our ultimate good. God is at work in all things for those who love Him and are called according to His purpose (Rom. 8:28 NIV). There were also times when the Holy Ghost forewarned Paul that trouble was ahead, yet he was to go. God's grace was more than sufficient to bring Paul through each trial.

Some would say here that God made Paul go through a trial. God led Paul to preach the gospel; the trial was the devil's resistance to the message. Paul overcame. Why? Because, Jesus said that He already overcame all the trials. God desires that we grow spiritually and advance in spreading His gospel. This alone will bring many trials your way. The enemy is completely arrayed against the plan of God. He wants to destroy it and defame God's Word.

So then, we are the objects of the devil's wrath, for we

are the objects of God's love. Through the church the message will reach the masses of people who haven't heard that God has made provision for their salvation. In James 1:2-5 we read, "Consider it pure joy, my brothers, whenever you face trials of many kinds, because you know that the testing of your faith develops perseverance. Perseverance must finish its work so that you may be mature and complete, not lacking anything" (NIV).

Jesus was strong enough, mature enough and complete in God to handle anything that evil resistance could throw His way. He could even die on the cross and on the third day rise again to defeat death itself. Jesus progressed to this ultimate place of invincibility. Our journey is ahead of us. Of course, it is a great comfort to know that someone already completed the course flawlessly.

Christ is the Alpha and the Omega. He has already been where you are going and prepared a safe place of refuge for you (John 14). When you journey into your future with Jesus, you will have the faith, hope, love, strength and courage to accomplish everything He has destined for you. Not only has He prepared a place for you to succeed, He has also prepared you with all you need to go forward in victory.

DISASTERS & CRISES

WHEN YOU JOURNEY INTO YOUR FUTURE WITH JESUS, YOU WILL HAVE THE FAITH, HOPE, LOVE, STRENGTH AND COURAGE TO ACCOMPLISH EVERYTHING HE HAS DESTINED FOR YOU.

When someone lifts weights, the resistance from the weights helps to grow and strengthen muscles. Without this resistance there is no exercise. We are to exercise ourselves unto godliness, which simply means, that our time in God's presence and His Word must be acted on. There are some things we act on that will be peaceful in our time of devotion to God. And then there will be an action of faith in the midst of resistance to our faith.

If you love God, know this. The devil is your adversary. He will put obstacles in your path and resist you at every turn. The devil resists us through sickness, disease, and poverty, difficulty in the home, depressions of all kinds, thoughts used against our faith, trials of many varieties involving other people, and certainly the resistance against our success in God.

But the enemy's resistance doesn't weaken us. We grow stronger. The joy of the Lord is our strength. As we persist and persevere, being strong and courageous in Christ, we grow stronger. Ultimately, we know the enemy is defeated. He was, and he is defeated through the victory of Jesus on the cross. We win!

Disasters & Crises
As we persist and persevere, being strong and courageous in Christ, we grow stronger. Ultimately, we know the enemy is defeated. He was, and he is defeated through the victory of Jesus on the cross. We win!

The majority of the things we have covered thus far are under the blood and were defeated by the death, burial and resurrection of the Lord. Yet as we have briefly mentioned, there are some things when other people become involved that are not as simple to define. Yes, there is much disaster in the world. As a result of this, the majority of people who will not listen to God, or incorporate any godly principles into their lives, become walking time bombs of disaster.

Our relationship with God sees us through every circumstance. Regardless of what anyone else does, we as children of God have immunity from self inflicted pain. If we are ordered to violate our conscience, there may be difficulties we incur that could have been avoided. God is merciful! You can count on Him to lead you safely to shore.

Many wonderful people were killed in the terrorist activities in our country in recent times. And many things are happening all over the world at an increasing and alarming rate. The signs of the times are accurate with Scripture as a preliminary to the coming of the Lord. These times will increase, not decrease. Yet in all the devastation, the grace of God will also increase to provide the divine ability to overcome.

Let's take an example from the Apostle Paul's life. Paul was a man of God who received direct revelation from the Lord concerning the redemption of mankind. If there were any revelation that the enemy doesn't want known, it is this. He lost the war when Jesus triumphed over him in the death, burial and resurrection. The last thing he wants is for anyone to find out what is available to any believer through the work of the Lord.

Satan loses when someone receives Jesus as Lord. And he loses again if they find out how wonderful their salvation is that they just received. Paul had a commission to reveal this wonder to the world. Do you think that Satan saw Paul as a primary target? Look at what Paul said about all the difficulties and disasters that he faced in his life up to this point:

> *Are they Hebrews? So am I. Are they Israelites? So am I. Are they the seed of Abraham? So am I. Are they ministers of Christ? — I speak as a fool — I am more: in labors more abundant, in stripes above measure, in prisons more frequently, in deaths often. From the Jews five times I received forty stripes minus one. Three times I was beaten with rods; once I was stoned; three times I was shipwrecked; a night and a day I have been in the deep; in journeys often, in perils of waters, in perils of robbers, in perils of my own countrymen, in perils of the Gentiles, in perils in the city, in perils in the wilderness, in perils in the sea, in perils among false brethren; in weariness and toil, in sleeplessness often, in hunger and thirst, in fastings often, in cold and nakedness — besides the other things, what comes upon me daily: my deep concern for all the churches. 29 Who is weak, and I am not weak? Who is made to stumble, and I do not burn with indignation?*
>
> (2 Corinthians 11:22-33)

Just reading this passage of Scripture will wear you out. Why was Paul's life so filled with turmoil? Paul answers this question in chapter twelve.

It is doubtless not profitable for me to boast. I will come to visions and revelations of the Lord: I know a man in Christ who fourteen years ago — whether in the body I do not know, or whether out of the body I do not know, God knows — such a one was caught up to the third heaven. And I know such a man — whether in the body or out of the body I do not know, God knows — how he was caught up into Paradise and heard inexpressible words, which it is not lawful for a man to utter. Of such a one I will boast; yet of myself I will not boast, except in my infirmities. For though I might desire to boast, I will not be a fool; for I will speak the truth. But I refrain, lest anyone should think of me above what he sees me to be or hears from me.

And lest I should be exalted above measure by the abundance of the revelations, a thorn in the flesh was given to me, a messenger of Satan to buffet me, lest I be exalted above measure. Concerning this thing I pleaded with the Lord three times that it might depart from me. And He said to me, "My grace is sufficient for you, for My strength is made perfect in weakness." Therefore most gladly I will rather boast in my infirmities, that the power of Christ may rest upon me. Therefore I take pleasure in infirmities, in reproaches, in needs, in persecutions, in distresses, for Christ's sake.

For when I am weak, then I am strong.
(2 Corinthians 12:1-10)

The revelation of the Lord Jesus Christ was the very reason why Satan hounded the tracks of the Apostle Paul. If he could keep Paul from revealing the truth, then many would perish through ignorance. We see this same ploy during the Dark Ages, where the Word of God was kept from the ordinary person. Very little light was seen during those times until a man by the name of Martin Luther discovered that the "just shall live by faith."

And once again, God's Word began to grow in the hearts of men and woman. Could we conclude that the Dark Ages meant that God left the scene? Or was it the resistance of a few inspired by the devil that intentionally left humanity ignorant? Man is always the cause of man not seeing God. Whenever someone believes God, pay attention! God will be revealed.

The Lord told Paul that the grace of God was sufficient for the situations that he encountered. This could mean, at times, that God would sustain Paul as he went through a tough time. And it also meant that God was the deliverer who would either help Paul avoid disaster or triumph over it. The trial is not God. The temptation is not God. Neither is the persecution God. In all these things, we are overcomers!

Remember, it is not God who brings calamity. God didn't create the problem; He created the answer—faith in His Word. Whatever man allows, either through his adherence to the Word of God or his neglect of godliness, will produce results. There are good or bad consequences for every action. God's method of operation is to deal with people and their sin through the blood of Jesus, and to send laborers to inspire righteousness so that adversity can be avoided. God is merciful, way beyond the difficulties we encounter in life. God sent Jesus to stand in the gap for our mercy, and now He ever lives to intercede on our behalf, before He allows retribution. Listen to the truths of God's Word:

Disasters & Crises
Remember, it is not God who brings calamity. God didn't create the problem; He created the answer — faith in His Word.

Who is a God like You,
Pardoning iniquity
And passing over the transgression of the remnant of His heritage?

He does not retain His anger forever,
Because He delights in mercy.
He will again have compassion on us,
And will subdue our iniquities. (Micah 7:18-19)

If we are not careful, our interpretation of the Bible will make God to look like He afflicts one moment and blesses the next. It would be difficult to have any faith or trust in God if we were so clueless concerning God's character. God is not moody. He is consistent throughout the ages. He never varies. Either He is good or He is bad. He cannot be two personalities at the same time. God speaks of Himself through James when He presents the argument that salt water and fresh water cannot come out of the same tap. Good and bad cannot come from the same source.

God neither creates evil or does He support it. He never partners with the devil He defeated. God's judgment was the sentence placed on Jesus for the world's sin, which He fulfilled in His death, burial and resurrection. The ultimate judgment will come at the close of all things, called the, Great White Throne Judgment. This is where God will separate those who have been born again and those who have not. God calls this separation, "dividing the sheep from the goats." The judgment passed will involve one thing — the decision of man.

Choices
Choices are something that we make every day. The right ones will bring great blessing. The wrong choices will bring the sentence of the curse that is in the earth.

It's very interesting to understand how man decides his own fate. Choices are something that we make every day. The right ones will bring great blessing. The wrong ones will bring the sentence of the curse that is in the earth.

So let's remind ourselves again, where does God fit in when there are disasters, tribulation and trials? God fits into our lives in every conceivable place we will allow Him to.

Our choices will empower His Lordship over our lives, to give us protection, deliverance, soundness and safety all the days of our lives.

CHAPTER 4

Is God Hiding?

Hear, O LORD, when I cry with my voice!
Have mercy also upon me, and answer me.
When You said, "Seek My face,"
My heart said to You, "Your face, LORD, I will seek."

Do not hide Your face from me;
Do not turn Your servant away in anger;
You have been my help;

Do not leave me nor forsake me,
O God of my salvation.
When my father and my mother forsake me,
Then the LORD will take care of me.

(Psalm 27:7-10)

Does God ever hide from us? Or is it you and I who are hiding from Him? Especially when we act in ways that transgress His ways? In the Garden of Eden, when Adam and Eve sinned, they were questioned by God concerning their actions. Adam blamed Eve. Eve blamed the serpent. That started humanity's downslide of blame that has been coursing through history to the present.

Typically when people experience difficulty without any hope of change, blame is often the escape hatch. Isn't it interesting that with all the natural catastrophes, God gets blamed? The world calls hurricanes, tornadoes, cyclones, volcanoes and earthquakes all *acts of God*.

One morning in a town where I was holding a meeting, I decided to play golf. For a few holes I played alongside another golfer. We were near the green when he made another bad swing. The ball didn't go anywhere near where he intended for it to go. As you might imagine, profanity was flying. He began to damn God for his horrible golf swing. I walked up to him and asked, "Have you ever thought about blaming your swing on Buddha? Why don't you damn him?" I coached him to say "Buddha damn-it" a few times and then asked him how it felt.

Then I proceeded to take advantage of a stunned golfer who in his wildest imagination would never have thought that he would have a conversation like the one he was having. "Why did you blame God for your poor golf shot?"

I asked him if he considered God to be a good God. "Would God really cause your golf game to be poor?" I inquired. I asked him if he believed that he could approach God in a positive way and receive help for whatever he needed. Of course, this allowed me to tell him my profession, and when I said that I was a preacher, he apologized. For a few extra minutes I shared how God loved us so much that He sent His Son to die for our sins, to prove to everyone that He was *for* us and not *against* us. He didn't receive the Lord that day, but I believe that the Word of God will produce a harvest in his life. I'm sure you have been around people who without thinking have made their personal battles God's fault. Don't hide behind your own failures and sins by blaming God!

Stop Blaming God

It's surprising that so many Christians are mad at God about something. At times while praying with the sick, the Holy Spirit has revealed to me that they have resentment against God. A change in attitude must happen before that person can receive from God.

I believe that God is so good that even when resentments build up in an individual, God is not angry. We simply have a hard time receiving from God when a wall of resentment goes up between God and us. We think that He's hiding from us.

Resentment

I believe that God is so good that even when resentments build up in an individual, God is not angry. We simply have a hard time receiving from God when a wall of resentment goes up between God and us.

The truth is: God is simply on the other side of the wall we built. We are the ones who are hiding behind our own walls. So, we can't understand "where God fits in" because we can't see Him from behind the barriers we constructed of unfulfilled expectations, unresolved anger, unhealed hurts, and ungrateful attitudes.

Where is God? Too often, we push Him away and force a wall up between God and ourselves. How about you? Are you in hiding?

In Judges chapter six, we meet a man named Gideon who tried to put God behind a wall of blame:

> *Now the Angel of the LORD came and sat under the terebinth tree which was in Ophrah, which belonged to Joash the Abiezrite, while his son Gideon threshed wheat in the winepress, in order to hide it from the Midianites. And the Angel of the LORD appeared to him, and said to him, "The LORD is with you, you mighty man of valor!"*
>
> *Gideon said to Him, "O my lord, if the LORD is with us, why then has all this happened to us? And where are all His miracles which our fathers told us about, saying, 'Did not the LORD bring us up from Egypt?' But now the LORD has forsaken us and delivered us into the hands of the Midianites."*
>
> *Then the LORD turned to him and said, "Go in this might of yours, and you shall save Israel from the hand of the Midianites. Have I not sent you?"*
>
> *So he said to Him, "O my Lord, how can I save Israel? Indeed my clan is the weakest in Manasseh, and I am the least in my father's house."*

And the LORD said to him, "Surely I will be with you, and you shall defeat the Midianites as one man."
(Judges 6:11-16)

As we look at this passage, we are informed that the Midianites are enslaving the Israelites. We find Gideon hiding in the wine press and threshing wheat. As we will see, Gideon has had much time to formulate his opinion of the *LORD*. Notice that the *LORD* says that He is with Gideon, and yet Gideon responds that the *LORD* has forsaken Israel.

The *LORD* made it personal for Gideon, but Gideon jumped behind a wall of blame and projected his problem on Israel. Some of us have a difficult time considering that the *LORD* would use us personally, especially if the camp or circle we are in is not having experiences with God. I believe that in the earth today, we have already entered into a window of opportunity for anyone who would challenge the status quo. The things that we want changed are always easier to imagine if God Himself or someone else important, not us, does the unthinkable.

If history were to repeat itself, then the great majority of Christians will wait for a small minority to brave the odds of change. Of course, they will view and criticize from a safe distance. In Matthew 14:29 remember how many disciples were left in the boat when Peter braved to walk on the water? That's right, eleven. This means 92 per cent would rather watch than act and these were disciples — the leaders, the preachers if you will. WOW!

What would the percentages be if we considered the rest of all believers? If the preachers are the ones to demonstrate the virtues and blessings of God and only 8 per cent of them will dare to seek change with a willingness to act, then how will the sheep respond with any greater boldness?

Remember, the *LORD* addresses His statements directly to Gideon. He is assuring Gideon that He is with him. If Gideon understood that the Angel of the *LORD* was speaking God's irrefutable truth to him, he might have received it differently. As it is, he obviously doesn't know to whom he is talking. Isn't it true that if we only knew that the people we were talking about were listening, we might be more careful about our conversation?

Notice that the name *LORD* is capitalized referring to the "I Am" or "Yahweh" name of God. This is the formal name of God revealed to Moses through the burning bush. Yet when Gideon responds to Him, he calls Him "Lord" which is "adonai" meaning "my Lord." It's an informal name for God and could also be used as a greeting to any human being. In other words, Gideon speaks to the *LORD* in an informal, casual, natural way, not as the *LORD* of heaven and earth, the Almighty, Omnipresent God for whom nothing is impossible. As a result, we get to hear what Gideon is really thinking. While he was threshing wheat in the winepress, he developed an attitude or opinion about what things looked like to him in the natural.

With God, See the Supernatural and Believe the Impossible

Seeing your circumstances from a natural perspective will not give you the boldness or courage you need to see where God fits into your present situation. For example, Gideon was so blinded by the natural that he couldn't imagine God using Him or the Israelites to overcome their problems and win a supernatural victory.

God's perspective was greater than Gideon's perspective. God saw Gideon in a completely different light than Gideon saw himself. The LORD stated that He is with Gideon and that Gideon is a mighty man of valor. This means that God viewed Gideon as a brave and mighty warrior of a force or army. It's obvious that this recognition of God did not compute with Gideon. God knows the end from the beginning, so His statement reveals the future for Gideon.

Focus
YOU HAVE TO BE CAREFUL DURING TOUGH TIMES THAT YOU KEEP YOUR THOUGHTS FOCUSED ON THE WORD OF GOD.

Even though Gideon did not acknowledge God's assertions, did his lack of understanding make the statements of God less true? God always sees things from His perspective. To God, Gideon is a mighty man of valor. God spoke to him as though Gideon had already defeated the Midianites.

Gideon questions whether or not the *LORD* is with us. He answered the part that he comprehended. He used the natural to make his deductions. To Gideon, the only sensible conclusion to the difficulty that Israel is incurring is that the LORD has forsaken them. What about your perspective in life? In all your circumstances and relationships, do you see your life only from the natural? Are God's supernatural acts missing from your life?

Like Gideon, are you missing what God wants to do in your life because you can only see the visible — the natural? The Apostle Paul writes in 2 Corinthians 4:18 that we are to look at the things that are unseen rather than being occupied with the seen realm. What is seen is temporary or subject to change. Why rely only on a natural worldview that changes constantly when you are privileged to have God's supernatural perspective?

You have to be careful during tough times that you keep your thoughts focused on the Word of God. Gideon let his reason focus on all kinds of natural scenarios. He could not imagine that God would do anything supernatural. Paul prays in Ephesians, "Now to Him who is able to do exceedingly abundantly above all that we ask or think, according to the power that works in us . . . " (Ephesians 3:20). The miracle-working, supernatural power of God working in us by His Spirit will accomplish things far beyond anything you can imagine or think in the natural!

God isn't hiding from you. But like Gideon, you may be hiding behind a wall of blame. Or, you may be totally lacking in His supernatural perspective on your situation.

Whatever the case may be, if you are limited and bound to the natural, you will never perceive "where God fits in" the present or future situations of your life.

Your Opinion Doesn't Matter — Only God's Opinion Matters!

As Gideon began to speak, we can see that he has a strong opinion shaped by his natural reasoning, understanding and perspective. Gideon responds to the *LORD* by accusing God of forsaking the children of Israel and refusing to manifest the signs and wonders that the children of Israel had known.

Does this kind of thinking sound familiar? So many today are seeking the signs and wonders of God. We have the opinion that if we can have a visitation from God we can finally do the work of the Lord. We pray and plead to God for what we don't see, as if God is withholding something from us. Listen closely to what I am saying. Seeking God diligently for all that we see demonstrated in the Word is only right and proper. Praying fervently for the plan of God and its fulfillment is also a key ingredient to the will of God. Hungering for a visitation of God is the zeal and passion of God. So what am I saying?

The elements of seeking God, praying fervently and hungering for His best, are all categorized as a part of our relationship to God. Our diligence to do the work of the Lord right now is exercised through our faith and acceptance of our responsibility as in the Great Commission

(Matthew 28:18-20). God never intended for the church to do anything but respond to His instructions. When my instructions are clear and precise, I don't need any further discussion from my children. I just need their cooperation. Obedience is a wonderful thing. Tremendous results are produced as people obey instructions.

Your Opinions

Too often we pray selfishly. Our wants and opinions are at this point irrelevant to God.
Begin to pray and believe God for what is revealed in His Word — then obey.

Gideon wanted to argue with God, express his opinions, instead of simply seeing by faith God's perspective and acting by faith in obedience to what God wanted. Too often we pray selfishly. Our wants and opinions are at this point irrelevant to God. Begin to pray and believe God for what is revealed in His Word — then obey.

Take Responsibility for What God Asks You to Do

It will be good at this point to further see how God dealt with Gideon and his opinions concerning God's involvement. Verse 14 reads, "Then the LORD turned to him and said, "Go in this might of yours, and you shall save Israel from the hand of the Midianites. Have I not sent you?" Before we look at the first sentence, let's review the sentence, "Have I not sent you?" God was giving Gideon the responsibility to act and deliver Israel from the hands of the Midianites.

The *LORD* recognized the way Gideon had ignored the emphasis He placed on the deliverance of the Israelites as being in the hands of Gideon. So He reiterated and emphasized it again by saying, "Have I not sent you?" This certainly rocked Gideon's boat! His wall of blame was about to crumble. His opinions and arguments were of no effect. Gideon's natural worldview must have been shattered. He definitely realized his lack of respect for the Angel of the LORD.

In Verse 15 Gideon starts out his remarks by honoring the *LORD* for who He is. He replied to the Angel of the Lord, "How can I save Israel . . . ?" Now it can be very difficult to understand what God is saying to us when our perspective is clouded with religion or tradition. Paul prayed very earnestly for the church to have open eyes and God-given revelation to walk in the grace that was given. It seems to Paul that unless the church has eyes to see, then the fullness of their redemption will be ignored. Gideon's supernatural insight comes at this point; the responsibility to move in the miraculous and see the invisible becomes clear. He accepts and obeys God's will for his life.

God's Power is Available to You Now!

Go back to verse 14 and let's look at the beginning sentence. The LORD said, "Go in this might of yours, and you shall save Israel from the hands of the Midianites." Look closely at this phrase: *Go in this might of yours.*

God is revealing to Gideon the presence and power of God that had always been available to the children of Israel and to Gideon. In other words, God's call on the children of Israel came with the ability of God to accomplish the will of God for their lives. God would never withdraw His ability, yet man can willingly withdraw from God at any time. God is seeking a relationship, not avoiding one. He wants to meet with us face to face as a friend, like He did with Moses. God never hides from us.

God's Friend

God is seeking a relationship, not avoiding one. He wants to meet with us face to face as a friend, like He did with Moses. God never hides from us.

What Gideon didn't realize, until that encounter with the Angel of the Lord, was that the power of God, as with all miracles and wonders, is available to any man who willingly and faithfully will take up the cause for the heart of God. Right here is where we could miss it. As I said previously, believing God for a wave, or a move of God, and hungering for more of God is not wrong, unless it encompasses your lack of initiative for what can be done right now.

Redemption has provided everything necessary for your success. Obtaining all that God has for us does not mean that it is not available now. The level of spiritual attainment we have grown and developed in produces the demonstrations we are able to perform. Paul wrote in Romans 12:6, "We have different gifts, according to the grace given us. If a man's gift is prophesying, let him use it in proportion to his faith" (NIV).

Prophesying in proportion to our faith means to the level that we have used our faith. It would be easy to interpret this to mean that one is given more faith than another. Therefore, the level of prophesying is different. However, faith is the same, and is all given by God to be used with the optimum level of grace provided. In the end, God wants you to prophesy just like it was God Himself speaking. The grace is measured out for that specific area in which you will prophesy.

So, when we see an individual prophesying, the power and strength of God's words, relayed to the people, has much influence in the development of the individual prophesying. Whatever level they prophesy from does not mean that it is all the grace that's available. As they grow and mature and continue to yield to the Holy Ghost, they will increase in the things of God. Likewise, where we see Israel, when Gideon is threshing wheat in the winepresses, does not reflect the power and ability of Almighty God. He is not hiding.

Where does God fit in? He's there but He only acts according to the level that Gideon and Israel are yielded to Him. The eyes of the LORD are constantly roaming throughout the whole earth in search of loyalty and surrender. God desires vessels who willingly yield themselves to the will of God and courageously step into the unknown with the confidence of God's Word to back them up. Many things could be accomplished if men and women would only cooperate with the heart of God.

In my business class in high school, we learned about the concept called "supply and demand." The simplified version is this: where there is great demand for a product, there must of necessity be great supply to meet that demand. When there is great supply and little demand, you will see cost reductions. The retailers are endeavoring to liquidate their supply. However, when merchandise is not sold, there is loss incurred.

WILLING TO YIELD
GOD DESIRES VESSELS WHO WILLINGLY YIELD THEMSELVES TO THE WILL OF GOD AND COURAGEOUSLY STEP INTO THE UNKNOWN WITH THE CONFIDENCE OF GOD'S WORD TO BACK THEM UP. MANY THINGS COULD BE ACCOMPLISHED IF MEN AND WOMEN WOULD ONLY COOPERATE WITH THE HEART OF GOD.

The reverse situation: there is great demand, yet a small supply. In this case, the price is raised without concern of any loss. When the demand is great enough, people will wait in line and pay any price to get what they desire. I'm very confident that what God was explaining to Gideon had to do with the "supply" of the *LORD*. When the Angel of the *LORD* called Gideon a mighty man of valor, although this statement didn't look true, it was. This is because the supply of God's might was available for Gideon. However, Gideon didn't experience this until he was satisfied that God would fight for him.

When Gideon stepped out to perform, he stepped into God's supply. Whether Gideon felt anointed or not, when the Angel of the *LORD* said, "Go in this might of yours," the anointing for power was supplied to accomplish God's plan.

Gideon begins to see the importance of the *LORD's* statements, because now he tries to back out of the responsibility. Responsibility is a big word, isn't it? Do you think we are any different than the many heroes of faith from the past? Everyone is always glad and excited about a job well done as long as they were not responsible for it while it was being done. There is, however, a responsibility given to each believer to understand and acknowledge the ability of God in every arena of life.

In verse 15, Gideon said to the Lord, "O my Lord, how can I save Israel? Indeed my clan is the weakest in Manasseh, and I am the least in my father's house." You will find this same mentality in other passages of Scripture where God is calling men or women to a position of leadership. The feeling of inadequacy causes Gideon to endeavor to convince God that He is making the wrong choice. Gideon does everything he can to prove himself unworthy for the job. If we were to think about it from God's perspective, anyone under the old covenant would be considered unworthy, due to unredeemed sin, for a partnership with God.

However, God doesn't rely on the worthiness of Gideon to produce the miraculous. God doesn't rely on your worthiness in order to accomplish what He wills. Rather, God is positioning Gideon to where the ability of God is released through Gideon's faith and obedience to supersede the natural. Gideon simply needs to align himself with God's supernatural perspective.

Often, we try to get God to see our situation from our perspective. The truth is, we need to see ourselves and everything or everyone around us from His perspective.

In the new covenant in Christ, God positioned us — by the new birth — in the ability of God where the natural is superseded continually by the supernatural. The man or woman who acknowledges this through faith will live in this realm.

Verse 16 is one of my favorite verses in this passage. And the LORD said to him, "Surely I will be with you, and you shall defeat the Midianites as one man." There are two parts to this verse. First, "surely I will be with you", and second, "you shall defeat the Midianties as one man."

In the next two chapters, we will discuss these important statements that prophesy our future as new covenant believers. As we conclude this chapter, let's remember this essential truth:

God will never call us to do anything where
He hasn't already supplied the ability and the answers.

In other words, with God's call comes the supply. God's will is already established in heaven. His desire is for everything on earth to look like it does in heaven. What Gideon finally grasped is what we must also understand and act upon by faith. God waits on humanity to see and comprehend the tremendous blessings that await those who will walk by faith.

The ability of God isn't stumbled upon. There must be a conscious decision to walk with God. Even when the decision is made, it still might look in the natural like the odds are against you. However, when you engage and release God with your faith to get involved and take responsibility as He so desires, you have then accessed your answer, stepped into your supply, and seen clearly *where God fits in*. Glory to God!

CHAPTER 5

God *Is* With You

Matthew 1:23

"Behold, the virgin shall be with child, and bear a Son, and they shall call His name Immanuel," which is translated, "God with us."

How significant do you think the name Immanuel is to the plan of God that Jesus was to walk? Everything in the ministry of Jesus, as well as anyone who accomplished anything for God, had one thing in common. God was there!

What happens when God fits into our request for His presence? Part of the answer lies in Habakkuk 3:2-4:

O LORD, I have heard Your speech and was afraid;
O LORD, revive Your work in the midst of the years!
In the midst of the years make it known;
In wrath remember mercy.

God came from Teman,
The Holy One from Mount Paran.
Selah

His glory covered the heavens,
And the earth was full of His praise.
His brightness was like the light;
He had rays flashing from His hand,
And there His power was hidden.

As we can see, the prophet prays for God to revive His work and make His mercy known. Verse three is the answer: *God came.* When God gets on the scene, notice the description. "His glory covered the heavens, and the earth was full of His praise. His brightness was like the light; He had rays flashing from His hand, And there His power was hidden." As always, when God is present, every conceivable possibility of failure is removed.

Trusting in God throughout the ages has never disappointed those involved. On the contrary, everywhere God goes, He leaves a trail of the supernatural. I'm reminded of one such instance in the lives of the children of Israel as they were crossing the desert. The people of Israel came to Mount Sinai and God showed up. Notice the description:

Then it came to pass on the third day, in the morning, that there were thunderings and lightnings, and a thick cloud on the mountain; and the sound of the trumpet was very loud, so that all the people who were in the camp trembled. And Moses brought the people out of the camp to meet with God, and they stood at the foot of the mountain. Now Mount Sinai was completely in smoke, because the LORD descended upon it in fire.

Its smoke ascended like the smoke of a furnace, and the whole mountain quaked greatly. And when the blast of the trumpet sounded long and became louder and louder, Moses spoke, and God answered him by voice. Then the LORD came down upon Mount Sinai, on the top of the mountain. And the LORD called Moses to the top of the mountain, and Moses went up.
(Exodus 19:16-20)

In verse 17 is the reason why God enveloped the mountain. He was going to allow the children of Israel to meet Him. God really had no other agenda. Yet with just His presence being there, the mountain began to shake as thunder and lightning struck. The psalmist said in Psalm 97:5, "The mountains melt like wax at the presence of the LORD, At the presence of the Lord of the whole earth. The heavens declare His righteousness, And all the peoples see His glory."

Our God is an awesome God! Just His presence alone could make a mountain melt. What if God were actually defending us? As you could imagine, the children of Israel had a healthy respect for the power of God. Yet they certainly tried His patience and His mercy.

This brings us to a very interesting observation concerning the people of Israel. Throughout their history they had known of God's greatness. His powerful assistance, over and over again, was left etched in the minds of His people that if God was there; you had nothing to worry about. Granted, anyone can be full of doubt and unbelief. Like the children of Israel, as they marched out of Egypt and crossed the desert, they continually murmured and complained. Incredible miracles of protection and provision were common during their deliverance, yet they tested God with their unbelief.

You cannot expect everyone to rally behind the miraculous, even if it is right before their eyes. There is just enough devil or unbelief in some people, that no matter what God does, they refuse to believe. However, God has and will always have a remnant of people through which He can move and show Himself to be strong. From Genesis to Revelation, you can chart the course of those who believed in the miraculous of God. One common denominator of the miraculous always exists: God is present and the people know Him!

THE MIRACULOUS

YOU CANNOT EXPECT EVERYONE TO RALLY BEHIND THE MIRACULOUS, EVEN IF IT IS RIGHT BEFORE THEIR EYES. THERE IS JUST ENOUGH DEVIL OR UNBELIEF IN SOME PEOPLE, THAT NO MATTER WHAT GOD DOES, THEY REFUSE TO BELIEVE.

A great story that helps us to understand the mindset of the Israelites concerning the presence of God is found in 2 Samuel 6:1-23:

> *Again David gathered all the choice men of Israel, thirty thousand. And David arose and went with all the people who were with him from Baale Judah to bring up from there the ark of God, whose name is*

called by the Name, the LORD of Hosts, who dwells between the cherubim. So they set the ark of God on a new cart, and brought it out of the house of Abinadab, which was on the hill; and Uzzah and Ahio, the sons of Abinadab, drove the new cart. And they brought it out of the house of Abinadab, which was on the hill, accompanying the ark of God; and Ahio went before the ark. Then David and all the house of Israel played music before the LORD on all kinds of instruments of fir wood, on harps, on stringed instruments, on tambourines, on sistrums, and on cymbals.

And when they came to Nachon's threshing floor, Uzzah put out his hand to the ark of God and took hold of it, for the oxen stumbled.

Then the anger of the LORD was aroused against Uzzah, and God struck him there for his error; and he died there by the ark of God. And David became angry because of the LORD's outbreak against Uzzah; and he called the name of the place Perez Uzzah to this day. David was afraid of the LORD that day; and he said, "How can the ark of the LORD come to me?" So David would not move the ark of the LORD with him into the City of David; but David took it aside into the house of Obed-Edom the Gittite. The ark of the LORD remained in the house of Obed-Edom the Gittite three months. And the LORD blessed Obed-Edom and all his household.

Now it was told King David, saying, "The LORD

has blessed the house of Obed-Edom and all that belongs to him, because of the ark of God." So David went and brought up the ark of God from the house of Obed-Edom to the City of David with gladness. And so it was, when those bearing the ark of the LORD had gone six paces, that he sacrificed oxen and fatted sheep.

Then David danced before the LORD with all his might; and David was wearing a linen ephod. So David and all the house of Israel brought up the ark of the LORD with shouting and with the sound of the trumpet.

Now as the ark of the LORD came into the City of David, Michal, Saul's daughter, looked through a window and saw King David leaping and whirling before the LORD; and she despised him in her heart. So they brought the ark of the LORD, and set it in its place in the midst of the tabernacle that David had erected for it.

Then David offered burnt offerings and peace offerings before the LORD. And when David had finished offering burnt offerings and peace offerings, he blessed the people in the name of the LORD of hosts. Then he distributed among all the people, among the whole multitude of Israel, both the women and the men, to everyone a loaf of bread, a piece of meat, and a cake of raisins. So all the people departed, everyone to his house.

Then David returned to bless his household. And

> *Michal the daughter of Saul came out to meet David, and said, "How glorious was the king of Israel today, uncovering himself today in the eyes of the maids of his servants, as one of the base fellows shamelessly uncovers himself!"*
>
> *So David said to Michal, "It was before the LORD, who chose me instead of your father and all his house, to appoint me ruler over the people of the LORD, over Israel. Therefore I will play music before the LORD. And I will be even more undignified than this, and will be humble in my own sight. But as for the maidservants of whom you have spoken, by them I will be held in honor."*
>
> *Therefore Michal the daughter of Saul had no children to the day of her death.*

As their king, David was entrusted with the overall goodwill of his people. There was no king who cared for his people that would on purpose fail to make provision and protection for them. The greatest thing that King David could do for the children of Israel was to facilitate a place for the presence of God — the ark of the covenant. To the people of God, the moment the ark was once again in Israel's possession all would be well. God's presence was represented in the ark of the covenant — the place of His dwelling under the old covenant.

The Blessing of His Presence

Everything represented in this story of the ark of the

covenant is prophetic unto the new covenant. God would improve the new covenant, as a replacement for the old, by making available His presence to dwell in the human heart through the shed blood of the Lord Jesus Christ.

When Jesus died on the cross, the veil of the temple was rent from the top to the bottom. God's presence came out of the ark of the covenant, a place made with human hands. Through the death, burial and resurrection, those who accept the finished work of Jesus Christ become the human temple of the Lord. God has come to dwell in our hearts and to live through our lives!

Talk about drawing near, you can't get any closer to God than our redemption that Jesus bought for you and me. If the Israelites were excited about bringing a *box* into their possession because God was in it, then how much more excited should we be? God is in us!

God's Nearness
If the Israelites were excited about bringing a *box* into their possession because God was in it, then how much more excited should we be? God is in us!

Do you see through this story how powerful the presence of the Lord is? Obed-Edom carried on as before, yet with one tremendous difference! God was there. Just the presence of God alone made all the difference in the world. God is the center of all blessings! He could not be cursed even if He tried. In His presence, blessings abound. But when we wall ourselves in and separate ourselves from His presence, we walk as in a curse.

When you respect who He is, you receive what He has. Blessings abounded in the home of Obed-Edom. King David took thirty thousand men with him to retrieve the ark and bring it back to the temple of God in Israel. As we can see from the story, the music was playing and people were shouting as the ark entered the City of David.

What a celebration! What gave rise to this celebration? The presence of God was once again in the company of the people of God. There were no reservations that day among those who knew and respected the awesomeness of God. King David himself danced before the Lord with all his might. Nothing was held back before the Lord. All of this was done just because the presence of God was now back in the midst of the children of God, and they would gain great benefit from the God they served. Here we see demonstrated a level of awe and respect for God that every one of us could learn from.

Putting Out a Fleece for God's Presence

Let's return to the story of Gideon. Even after receiving a direct message from God's angel and the assurance of God's presence, Gideon still wanted more validation of God's presence.

As we continue to look at Gideon, he definitely shows his belief in God's ability. Remember that Gideon said to the Angel of the LORD, "If the LORD is with us, then why has all this happened to us?" (Judges 6). Romans 8:31 reads, "What then shall we say to these things? If God is for us, who can be against us?" So, when God is for you, who can be against you? Gideon believed that if the LORD were involved with the children of Israel, then His presence would definitely eliminate the enemy.

Traditionally, when we think of Gideon, we associate him with the fleeces that he made to the LORD. Isn't it ironic how the flesh draws back from the anointing and resists the supernatural? God in His design of man specifically made the body for the anointing. Before sin was an issue to Adam, his flesh was in complete harmony with the supernatural. Now Gideon struggled with the idea of being the one whom God commissioned to move in supernatural strength. In desperation, he asked God for extra assurance until his confidence in God's presence was secure.

Gideon knew that there was no need to get overly aggressive about war, when God is not on your side. He also knew that the only thing capable of securing success was God. Gideon wanted to make absolutely sure that God would, in fact, be with him, and that the result of the conflict would be victorious. Once these issues were settled, Gideon became bold to accomplish God's assignment.

We might want to ask ourselves:

1. To what degree would you need to know that God was with you and that victory was secure?
2. Have these central issues been settled in our covenant?

Now to continue, I want you to consider the importance of these two issues as we look at the lives of some others who did great things through God's power. So, if you knew God was with you and you couldn't fail, would you still need a sign from God of His faithfulness?

CONFIDENCE IN GOD
SO, IF YOU KNEW GOD WAS WITH YOU AND YOU COULDN'T FAIL, WOULD YOU STILL NEED A SIGN FROM GOD OF HIS FAITHFULNESS?

God created man for His glory. Psalm 8:4-5 declares, "What are mortals that you should think of us, mere humans that you should care for us? For you made us only a little lower than God, and you crowned us with glory and honor" (NLT).

When man sinned and fell short of the glory of God, man began to lose consciousness of spiritual things. God removed Adam and Eve from the Garden of Eden. Sin became a *wall* between man and God's presence. Now we know that God did not disappear — His presence was still in the earth. If man were interested in cultivating a relationship with God, he could. However, it just wouldn't be the same as with God's original intention.

For instance, in Genesis 4, God worked with Cain to avoid the sin conceived in his heart. Because Cain still retained knowledge of the universal mind of God, he was very aware of the sound of God. Cain understood God completely as God gave warning of his desire for sin. God worked as well as he could within the framework of sin that was in the earth. Things became increasingly difficult as man drifted further from the knowledge of God. However, man has no excuse for his lack of knowledge of God, as Paul instructs us in Romans 1, for the beauty of nature itself reveals God.

The Power of Being in His Presence

If indeed man is brought up in a godless society, he can live and die without the desire for spiritual things. There is no doubt that within the heart of man lies a void for the intention of his existence. However, the distractions of life can not only dull the conscience of man, but also, divert the attention of man from seeking the spiritual answers he needs. Maybe this is why the story of Enoch is so impressive. He discovered the power of being in God's presence.

> *When Enoch had lived 65 years, he became the father of Methuselah. And after he became the father of Methuselah, Enoch walked with God 300 years and had other sons and daughters. Altogether, Enoch lived 365 years. Enoch walked with God; then he was no more, because God took him away* (Genesis 5:21-24 NIV).

Seven generations after Adam, Enoch arrives on the scene. We have limited information about him, yet the facts we do have reveal an individual who sought God without assistance. Can you think back seven generations to the thoughts and dreams of your ancestors? Most of us have no idea who our relatives were seven generations back. There must have been some information passed down through the generations concerning the mind of God. After 65 years Enoch stepped into a relationship with God that lasted 300 years.

Hebrews 11:6 records how Enoch developed the relationship. Remember, God never went anywhere when man sinned. He just lost His place in the heart of man where He no longer would be their priority. Verse six tells us that without faith it is impossible to please God. This is in reference to Enoch's relationship with God. We know that Enoch used faith to approach God. Verse six goes on to say, "He that comes to God must believe that He is and that He is a rewarder of those who diligently seek Him."

Pursuing a Relationship

How important is it to you that God is there and that with diligence you could develop a consistent walk with the Lord?

Faith was used by Enoch to believe that God existed. If everyone around Enoch had been walking with God, with the evidence of God's power, then Enoch wouldn't have had to believe that God is. However, as we can see here, Enoch was by himself as he approached God.

What did it mean to Enoch that God was there? The

only way to secure a relationship with God was to be sure that God was, and that He would respond to Enoch if he would diligently seek Him. How important is it to you that God is there and that with diligence you could develop a consistent walk with the Lord? The story of Enoch and the time he spent with God is a great encouragement to those of us who are developing our own relationship with the Lord.

God's Presence Instills Confidence and Courage

Now let's look at the confidence that was placed in the heart of a warrior on commission with God. Looking back at Moses and the call of God on his life, the presence of God was crucial to his acceptance of God's plan. Moses, like many others, tried to change God's mind about His choice. Everything was fine with Moses concerning God delivering His people from Egypt, until God wanted to use him. The statement that comforted Moses — God's promise to him, which was backed up with signs and wonders as proof, was, "I will certainly be with you."

Moses completely depended upon the power of God. As a very humble man, he was willing to yield to the greater ability of God. In Exodus 33:14-17 we read, "And He said, 'My Presence will go with you, and I will give you rest.' Then he said to Him, 'If Your Presence does not go with us, do not bring us up from here. For how then will it be known that Your people and I have found grace in Your sight, except You go with us? So we shall be separate, Your people and I, from all the people who are upon the face of the earth.' So the LORD said to Moses, 'I will also do this thing that you have spoken; for you have found grace in My sight, and I know you by name.'"

From Moses' example you can learn that without God you are helpless, yet in His power and strength you are invincible!

When Moses was ready to die, it was necessary that his mantle be passed on. The Lord chose Joshua as the next leader of the children of Israel. Moses was instructed by the Lord to have a ceremony, where Moses would lay his hands on Joshua and transfer the anointing upon him. After this event, we pick up Joshua's beginning days as leader in Joshua chapter one.

> *After the death of Moses the servant of the LORD, it came to pass that the LORD spoke to Joshua the son of Nun, Moses' assistant, saying: "Moses My servant is dead. Now therefore, arise, go over this Jordan, you and all this people, to the land which I am giving to them — the children of Israel. Every place that the sole of your foot will tread upon I have given you, as I said to Moses. From the wilderness and this Lebanon as far as the great river, the River Euphrates, all the land of the Hittites, and to the Great Sea toward the going down of the sun, shall be your territory. No man shall be able to stand before you all the days of your life; as I was with Moses, so I will be with you. I will not leave you nor forsake you.*

Be strong and of good courage, for to this people you shall divide as an inheritance the land which I swore to their fathers to give them. Only be strong and very courageous, that you may observe to do according to all the law which Moses My servant commanded you; do not turn from it to the right hand or to the left, that you may prosper wherever you go.

This Book of the Law shall not depart from your mouth, but you shall meditate in it day and night, that you may observe to do according to all that is written in it. For then you will make your way prosperous, and then you will have good success. Have I not commanded you? Be strong and of good courage; do not be afraid, nor be dismayed, for the LORD your God is with you wherever you go." (Joshua 1:1-9)

The Lord's instructions are too good to be true. Absolute success is guaranteed if Joshua adheres to the words of the Lord. Notice the encouragement and fortitude that comes through the message to Joshua. Every place that Joshua sets his foot will be his. How good is this? Do you think you would be up for the job if God promised you the same? Look at what God requires of Joshua.

Character. Then God asks Joshua to exhibit a certain character — be strong and of good courage.

Meditation. God reveals a secret to keeping the law. Meditation is the key. Meditate day and night so that everything you do will be with respect to the law and you will be guaranteed success.

Confident certainty. Then God reiterates again to Joshua to be strong and of good courage for the Lord is with you and will not forsake you. The anointing works when you tackle your problems with certainty.

Doesn't this encourage you? Think of the possibilities — if a man where backed by God and instructed like this! Friends, take advantage of God's provision and spend time with Him. Take time with this material. The old covenant pales in comparison with the new covenant. Joshua is not even in our league. These men were simply the servants of the Lord. Through the shed blood of Jesus, we are "sons of the living God." Paul says in the book of Romans, that we are heirs to the throne of God and joint heirs with Jesus. Everything spoken to Joshua is weak in comparison to the words of our new covenant.

Not that God is weak, but the strength of the covenant is weak compared to the new covenant. Does it make a difference that God is with us? How should this affect us?

God with Us Produces Amazing Results

If we were to discover that the presence of God is the defining reason why Jesus had success in His earth walk, would this convince us to embrace a more serious relationship with God? Peter defines the ministry of the Lord in Act 10:38, "How God anointed Jesus of Nazareth with the Holy Spirit and with power, who went about doing good and healing all who were oppressed by the devil, for God was with Him."

Getting Serious
If we were to discover that the presence of God is the defining reason why Jesus had success in His earth walk, would this convince us to embrace a more serious relationship with God?

With respect to our subject, notice the phrase, "For God was with Him." As a man, Jesus was inclined to produce results the same way any other human would. It was the anointing that Jesus walked in that produced the amazing results recorded in the gospels.

Let me reiterate to you that Immanuel means, "God is with us." This means that everywhere Jesus goes, God goes. There might not be a second thought to this statement when considering Jesus as the Son of God. But remember, according to Philippians 2, Jesus left His heavenly throne and humbled himself as a man. Jesus was the Son of Man. So, everywhere the man Jesus went, God went.

If you were unable to use the very thing that made you unique, then you wouldn't be unique. Jesus never stopped being God in the flesh. However, He couldn't use His power and authority as God. He laid these qualities down, so He would be subject to the earth as a man.

John the Baptist was baptizing in the river Jordan when Jesus walked up to him. As John saw Him approaching, he called out, "Behold, the Lamb of God which takes away the sin of the world." Then Jesus was baptized.

When all the people were baptized, it came to pass that Jesus also was baptized; and while He prayed, the heaven was opened. And the Holy Spirit descended in bodily form like a dove upon Him, and a voice came from heaven which said, "You are My beloved Son; in You I am well pleased." Now Jesus Himself began His ministry at about thirty years of age." (Luke 3:21-23)

Now Jesus began His ministry after He was baptized in the River Jordan. It was the Spirit of God that came upon Him, which authorized and empowered Him to launch out in ministry. His first miracle after His ordination is found in John chapter two. "When the master of the feast had tasted the water that was made wine, and did not know where it came from (but the servants who had drawn the water knew), the master of the feast called the bridegroom. And he said to him, 'Every man at the beginning sets out the good wine, and when the guests have well drunk, then the inferior. You have kept the good wine until now!' This beginning of signs Jesus did in Cana of Galilee, and manifested His glory; and His disciples believed in Him." (John 2:9-11)

For anyone who is willing to step out and minister, this passage about Jesus is a wonderful study of the anointing. Jesus was patient to wait for the anointing to come upon His life before setting out to heal and minister the Word of God. Later Jesus uses the results of this wonderful anointing to verify His position as the Son of God.

For Jesus to have the impact that He did, He would have to produce the results of the Father God. Jesus came as the Father's representative.

If we were to question how much Jesus relied upon the anointing, this would be the answer: *Everything that Jesus accomplished verified His relationship with the Father God.* Everything He would accomplish on the earth would be through the anointing. Jesus' empowerment and authority would reveal the heart of love that the Father has for His creation.

Had not the ministry of Jesus made the impact that it did upon the earth, there would be no one who would believe in Him after He arose from the grave. "For God was with Him" was evident in every word and action. Therefore, the world still stands in awe of the risen Savior.

VERIFICATION
EVERYTHING THAT JESUS ACCOMPLISHED VERIFIED HIS RELATIONSHIP WITH THE FATHER GOD.

As important as the presence of the Lord was to these men whom we have discussed, Jesus said before He went to the cross that there would be a time when He would no longer be on the earth. Yet Jesus said to the disciples that it would be to their advantage that He would leave them. When we see with amazement the results that normal men can have when God is on their side, then it becomes paramount that God be with us, too.

Jesus relied on the presence of the Father through the

Holy Spirit, so how could we make it without at least the same?

The Power of Presence Changed Peter

I'm reminded of the impact that Jesus had on one of the disciples named, Peter. We know that Peter was very impulsive, and for that reason he is very special to the gospels. What we do know is that Peter was very close to the Master. He was one of the inner three that learned more than the others. He was a leader in the midst of any situation. Quick to act — sometimes this was good and sometimes not. When Jesus preached and healed, there were many Pharisees and Sadducees who followed Him to find fault. They were very skeptical and always looked for cause to accuse Jesus.

More than once Jesus made these men so mad that they endeavored to throw Jesus over a hill to His destruction. Each time, Jesus simply walked right past them without being touched. To anyone standing by, like Peter, Jesus seemed indestructible.

Toward the end of the earthly ministry of Jesus, I see Peter do something that makes his companionship with Jesus even more powerful.

> *Then Judas, having received a detachment of troops, and officers from the chief priests and Pharisees, came there with lanterns, torches, and weapons. Jesus therefore, knowing all things that would come upon Him, went forward and said to them, "Whom are you seeking?"*

They answered Him, "Jesus of Nazareth."

Jesus said to them, "I am He." And Judas, who betrayed Him, also stood with them. Now when He said to them, "I am He," they drew back and fell to the ground.

Then He asked them again, "Whom are you seeking?"

And they said, "Jesus of Nazareth."

Jesus answered, "I have told you that I am He. Therefore, if you seek Me, let these go their way," that the saying might be fulfilled which He spoke, "Of those whom You gave Me I have lost none."

Then Simon Peter, having a sword, drew it and struck the high priest's servant, and cut off his right ear. The servant's name was Malchus.

So Jesus said to Peter, "Put your sword into the sheath. Shall I not drink the cup which My Father has given Me?" (John 18:2-11)

Why would Peter do such a thing? There are troops, hundreds of soldiers waiting to take Jesus. Why try to kill someone; it would be suicide? The only explanation would be that Peter is so extremely confident because of his association with Jesus.

In Scripture, we read over and over again of God informing a person in need that "He was with them," and the knowledge of His presence changed that person from being timid to becoming bold and courageous. Peter had never seen anyone take Jesus before.

Without fail, Jesus had avoided every confrontation of the Jewish leaders. I'm sure that Peter felt so secure that without thinking, he struck the servant of the high priest before he realized what he had done. Peter's spontaneous action was something that had become extremely big in him. The unsurpassable Christ was with him!

How quickly, though, things can change when your source of confidence leaves you. And Simon Peter followed Jesus, and so did another disciple. "Now that disciple was known to the high priest, and went with Jesus into the courtyard of the high priest. But Peter stood at the door outside. Then the other disciple, who was known to the high priest, went out and spoke to her who kept the door, and brought Peter in. Then the servant girl who kept the door said to Peter, 'You are not also one of this Man's disciples, are you?' He said, 'I am not.'" (John 18:15-17)

If you are familiar with this passage, you know that Peter denied the Lord three times. What happened to all his boldness? Is it possible that Peter's boldness was attached to his direct contact with the Lord? Well, Peter is not alone. From this time onward, we see that all the disciples showed fear and a lack of confidence. Even after Jesus' resurrection He had to rebuke the disciples for their unbelief.

Something remarkable happened that changed everything. On the day of Pentecost, the disciples, along with many others, were in the upper room praying when the

Holy Ghost came mightily upon them. Now, when Peter and the disciples were filled with the Holy Ghost, a new and fresh boldness entered them. Peter, the one who a few days before could not answer questions about his association with the Lord without denying Him, now stands up before thousands to proclaim the truth of the gospel.

What made the difference? The words, "For God was with him." The presence of the Holy Ghost in and upon the disciples empowered them to be bold witnesses for the Lord. God's presence filled them and fills us with boldness.

In the next few chapters, I will continue to build upon these thoughts. Our awareness of spiritual things and their familiarity will bless us with a great boldness in life. We should not experience any less than the disciples of the early church. We should have a greater experience! Though the world around us robs us of the awareness of our closeness to God that should be so natural in us.

Boldness
God's presence filled them and fills us with boldness.

As God helped the early church, He will help us. Jesus' last words were, "Lo, I'm with you always, even unto the end of the age." His abiding presence can change everything in our lives.

Be bold. Be courageous. You have nothing to fear. Jesus is Immanuel! He is with you!

CHAPTER 6

As One Man

And the LORD said to him, "Surely I will be with you, and you shall defeat the Midianites as one man." (Judges 6:16)

How can "one man" win a war? The Lord said to Gideon, "You shall defeat the Midianites as *one man*." Amazing!

In the last chapter, we learned that "God was with him [Gideon]." Throughout the chapter, we describe the significance of the phrase, "for God was with him." Our continuing question has been, "Where does God fit in?" We are discovering that whenever God's presence manifests in a situation or fills a person, remarkable and miraculous things begin to happen.

Imagine for a moment that you were one of the disciples following Jesus in the first century. What an awesome honor it would have been to see the marvelous display of God through the ministry of Jesus. Since Jesus was the divine expression of God in the flesh, the disciples were exposed to an accurate image of the Father

God. Jesus said to Phillip in John 14 that if he wanted to see the Father, he should look at what He, Jesus, accomplished. In seeing Jesus, Philip and the disciples understood the Father's ways. If believers could just see Jesus today, they would understand the Father's ways for them.

Those who struggle to understand the heart of our heavenly Father have never comprehended the significance of their position in Christ. Because they have a difficult time seeing Jesus and how He fits into their lives, they have a difficult time understanding how one man could defeat an army. Do we really recognize what it means to have "God with us?" Wouldn't it be wonderful to know that "God with us" was more than just His presence accompanying us as we continue to suffer through our difficulty? Could it be that God's presence would eliminate the suffering altogether?

We must understand an important truth. So much of our unbelief comes from misconceptions of God. What we have seen in the lives of men and women of God influences our understanding of a particular subject. When we see, however, that most Christians comfort one another without providing the necessary solution, then we unconsciously relate to God with the same conception. Thank God that His presence is life-changing. His presence shatters conventional wisdom. His presence reveals the Father and all that the Father has for us. Where the Spirit of the Lord is, there is liberty or the freedom to bring change.

God Works Through Us

The phrase, one man is prophetic to our dispensation. Throughout the Bible, God conveyed the message to fallen man that a union between God and man is what He desires. To God, working with and through a person is His avenue into the earth to effect change. For us, this incarnate relationship means success and an unlimited supply of God's ability.

God's intent for Adam was to rule this earth, as He, God, ruled all things. Certainly Adam would learn and develop as a mighty ruler of the earth. However, God might as well run things on earth if a person has to get instructions on every little thing that he does. On purpose, God constructed a being that could think and act like Himself.

When God turned everything over to Adam He didn't lose anything in the transition. Adam began by giving names to all the animals. God must have been pleased, because He never intervened with change. Adam must have tapped into the universal mind of God and used the full capacity of knowledge to do what he did as God would have done it.

Could such ability be given to man? Ability such that man is capable of operating his assignments on the earth as one with God? Man will never be independent of God.

Yet, could man become so intertwined in the thoughts and ability of God that he becomes divinely assertive throughout his life? Did God ever want man ill equipped or unprepared for the difficulties of life?

No, just the opposite is true. Before God formed Adam and breathed into his nostrils the breath of life, God made complete provision for His man. Redemption of man wouldn't be complete without God returning things to their original position or better. Provision has been made for man to step up and be a ruler in the earth, honoring and blessing God the Father with righteousness in every corner of the earth. Think of the implications if man where to rise up out of his slumber and begin to do things like God. Only with the ability of God Himself, of course! Man and God are to work together to accomplish the impossible.

Jesus was and is the greatest rule of measurement for the plan of God fulfilled. If someone were to ask Jesus, where does God fit in? He would say, In everything and everywhere. Jesus gave us a visible demonstration of a man completely connected to God. He was someone who laid down His life for others.

The Impossible
Man and God are to work together to accomplish the impossible.

Never did Jesus submit to the will of His flesh as mastery over the will of the Father God. Sure, the flesh of Jesus had a voice. It would tell Him of the basic needs like any other. Yet, Jesus never listened to the sinfulness of the world that used man's flesh as its vehicle. He stayed completely committed to the will of God.

In John 10, Jesus mentioned a great secret to His success, which demonstrated over and over again the Fathers intentions for man.

> *"I and the Father are one." Then again the Jewish leaders picked up stones to kill him. Jesus said, "At God's direction I have done many a miracle to help the people. For which one are you killing me?"*
>
> *They replied, "Not for any good work, but for blasphemy; you, a mere man, have declared yourself to be God."*
>
> *"In your own Law it says that men are gods!" he replied. "So if the Scripture, which cannot be untrue, speaks of those as gods to whom the message of God came, do you call it blasphemy when the one sanctif ed and sent into the world by the Father says, 'I am the Son of God'? Don't believe me unless I do miracles of God. But if I do, believe them even if you don't believe me. Then you will become convinced that the Father is in me, and I in the Father."* (John 10:30-38 TLB)

Jesus declared in verse 30, "I and my Father are one." Do you see the significance in these words in relationship to the Angel of the LORD's comments to Gideon? Gideon defeated the Midianites as one man — a position that the Lord convinced Gideon to assume.

Once God has a man or woman in a position where there's no difference between what God can do, and what the man or woman can do, then you have the miraculous. Remember, we should desire to see God in every area of our lives.

The Power to Do What God Wills

Moses had a tremendous encounter with God, which portrays this revelation even further. As we know, God had appeared to Moses in the burning bush. During this visitation with the Lord, God reveals to Moses that He sees the suffering and bondage of His people, Israel. He tells Moses that He will deliver them and set them free. Immediately following this statement, God tells Moses that He will use Moses. Of course, Moses' first response is like unto Gideon's response. In essence, he says, "Who me?" Moses unsuccessfully tells God why He is making the wrong choice. Once Moses accepts the job, (read Psalm 103:7) God begins to teach Moses how to work with Him to accomplish the mission.

God began with the first two miracles as a witness to His power, which Moses would learn to trust. After a long progression of signs and wonders, Egypt consents to let the children of Israel go. Every step God had Moses take was to be a step of development in Moses' consciousness. God's desire was for Moses to begin to think and act like Him.

A time of great testing came when the children of Israel came to the Red Sea. God actually expected Moses to know what to do. Even though the situation looked impossible, by this time and after months of teaching, Moses was ready for his first miracle where his command of faith would access the powers of God. Yet, we see Moses insist with flawless vigor that God would again set the children of Israel free.

> *And Moses said to the people, "Do not be afraid. Stand still, and see the salvation of the LORD, which He will accomplish for you today. For the Egyptians whom you see today, you shall see again no more forever. The LORD will fight for you, and you shall hold your peace."*
>
> *And the LORD said to Moses, "Why do you cry to Me? Tell the children of Israel to go forward. But lift up your rod, and stretch out your hand over the sea and divide it. And the children of Israel shall go on dry ground through the midst of the sea."*
>
> (Exodus 14:13-17)

The content of Moses' words to the children of Israel sounded impeccable, yet God heard them quite differently. Now here comes the rebuke from God to Moses. Remember, all this is a learning process where God is endeavoring to get Moses to conceptualize the thoughts of God. Verse 15 says, "Why do you cry to Me?" In other words, Moses is really waiting on God to do something that was in the ability of Moses to do.

In Exodus 7:1, God made Moses as God to Pharoah: "So the LORD said to Moses: 'See, I have made you as God to Pharaoh, and Aaron your brother shall be your prophet.'" This simply means that God expected Moses to do the job of delivering the people of Israel as if He were God. To think like God is to act like God. We have such an advantage today by having the written Word of God to study. We can enact the will of God in the earth!

God wanted Moses to recognize that the rod in His hand was just as powerful — if Moses used it according to God's plan — as if God Himself specifically told Moses to use it. Moses had to consider that there was no difference between him and God concerning this assignment. At the Red Sea, Moses and God were present. Even though there were two, God wanted Moses to believe that there was only one present. Which one was *the one*? They both were!

Faith Acts
To think like God is to act like God.

If Moses could have seen that there was no difference, perhaps he would have used the rod to split the sea without God's suggestion. This would have been the highest compliment to God, for now God has successfully taught a man to think like God. Ultimately, if God gave man the rule and ownership to the earth, then anything that God would suggest for man to consider would have been possible for that man whether God had suggested it or not.

Communion and Oneness with God

Remember, man is not independent of God, just one in essence and purpose. Communion with God, then, is not trying to find out what to do, because we don't have the capacity to comprehend the answer. Communion with God is the sweetest friendship between two who share the common desire to see the will of God for the earth fulfilled. It's a partnership and co-laboring in the work of God, each equally capable of handling whatever adversity comes with simplicity and ease.

Such oneness intends for God to work with man, and man to work with God. They become inseparable in nature, thought and deed.

Throughout his life, Jesus always had a tremendous respect for the will of His Father. Even in His youth, Jesus was concerned about His Father's business. We're not talking about His earthly father, Joseph. Jesus was in tune with His heavenly Father. Everything that has to do with the heavenly Father, involves accessing heaven to change the earth. Especially in the Gospel of John, we see that with every word Jesus spoke, He had accepted and comprehended the plan of God for His life.

When Jesus said that He came not to do His own will, but the will of the Father, He actually comprehended that He came from heaven on assignment to do the will of heaven. Jesus said elsewhere that He understood the voice of the Father because He was from above. Jesus was quoted more than once as saying that the words He spoke were not His own, but the words of His Father. He revealed that the deeds that He did were what He saw the Father do. All these statements reveal that Jesus was conscious of the Father, at the same time being aware of the flesh.

Jesus knew that He could speak and choose any words, yet He chose the words of His Father. When Jesus meditated and talked about His assignment, there was always Jesus and the Father. Yet, when Jesus fulfilled His assignment there was only Jesus. One time we see Jesus pray to the Father to work a miracle. At the tomb of Lazarus — Jesus prayed and said that His prayer was not for Himself, but for those who were standing by.

Purpose
God's purpose is to indwell you the same way He indwelt Christ.

God's purpose is to indwell you the same way He indwelt Christ. Paul writes, "To them God has chosen to make known among the Gentiles the glorious riches of this mystery, which is Christ in you, the hope of glory." (Colossians 1:27)

The Apostle Paul stands alone in history as the man to whom God revealed this great mystery. This mystery has been revealed to man as the central focus of redemption. Man coming into union with God! It was the shed blood and sacrifice of Jesus that provided this miracle.

God proved that it was possible when He made Adam and breathed into him the breath of life. Then Jesus, the Word of God, became flesh and dwelt among us. God was endeavoring to prove to man that union with deity was possible. Throughout the world, man has done many crazy things to fulfill himself like drugs, extreme sports, making great wealth, sexual excesses, etc. Many scholars, like Abraham Maslow, have written about the need humans have to find self-realization or fulfillment. Within man is an innate yearning to reach beyond himself and find completion and wholeness. That desire cannot be reached apart from God.

Man was made in the image of God for the glory of God. He was to inhabit the earth as a prince or ruler divinely connected to the source of life. All things being changed on account of sin, man has need of a divine connection in his heart.

The message the Apostle Paul was commissioned to preach would bring to man the understanding of our union with Christ. Paul persevered through great persecution to preach the revelation that he received from the Lord Jesus Christ. In Colossians 2:9-10, Paul says, "For in Christ there is all of God in a human body; so you have everything when you have Christ, and you are filled with God through your union with Christ. He is the highest Ruler with authority over every other power" (Living Bible).

This union can only be explained as we consider that there are two beings involved, God and you. The New Testament emphasizes this truth, explained in this way. For example, Jesus speaking to His disciples said in John 14:20, "At that day you will know that I am in My Father, and you in Me, and I in you."

Jesus was preparing His disciples to comprehend the ultimate purpose of redemption. We are not just trying to make it to heaven.

Redemption is God reproducing Himself in us, eliminating the sin nature and the curses that accompany sin. Everything that we used to be is swallowed up in the magnitude of God. Paul says in 2 Corinthians 5:17, "Therefore, if anyone is in union with Christ he is a new being; His old life has passed away, a new life has begun!" (20th Century).

Ephesians 2:10 continues to remind us of the radical change in our existence, "We are God's work of art, created in Christ Jesus to live the good life as from the beginning he had meant us to live" (Jerusalem). God revealed to Paul that two beings, God and man, could become one.

Later in Ephesians, Paul related this great mystery of the church to the union of marriage. God will reveal the truth of the Word of God through the natural courses of our lives. Marriage is understood as the merging of two lives into one. There are great benefits of two becoming one. Our resources are now doubled, our strengths are doubled and our efforts are now doubled. Everything should increase.

Likewise, in our relationship with God, everything immediately increases. Our whole life instantly becomes subjected to the greatness of what God is. Ephesians 1:3 says, "Let us give thanks to the God and Father of our lord Jesus Christ, for in our union with Christ he has blessed us by giving us every spiritual blessing in the heavenly world" (Good News).

Union is a word that a plumber understands. When two pipes are to come together, they must have a union to blend the halves. If the threads of the two pipes are opposite the other, there will be no joining unless a union is used. A union has the potential of merging opposite threads as though they were one. To understand the process, the mentioning of two pipes becoming one is necessary. Yet when the process is complete, the two pipes function as one pipe. There is no need while the work is being done to second guess which pipe gets more credit. They have become one in operation and the ability to supersede what they were before.

The plumber and the home owners are just glad that a connection has been made so ultimately the plumbing works, as it should.

Likewise, the Word of God is quite full of phrases, which mention man and God working together. For the purpose of understanding the connection and the expectation of the divine force of God working on our behalf, the two beings should consider each other. However when it comes to actually living by what we believe, the consideration of the heart switches to knowing that you have been equipped and strengthened for the task as one.

The reason why Paul says, "we are strong in the Lord and the power of His might," is so that we will valiantly

Doing the Impossible
I can do all things through Christ who strengthens me works when you realize that you can step out to do the miraculous and the impossible, knowing there is strength from Christ.

run to the giant as David did, knowing the real truth is that it is God running to the giant. *I can do all things through Christ who strengthens me* works when you realize that you can step out to do the miraculous and the impossible, knowing there is strength from Christ. The doing is easy and anointed when you know that everything you are is what He is!

Oneness with God Releases His Power

There never has been a believer who would bypass the ability of God, if they knew how to turn it loose. When it comes to magnifying God, be ever mindful of God's gracious plan, which made an allowance for every weakness in your life. As Paul said in Ephesians 2:15-18, "By abolishing in his flesh the law with its commandments and regulations. His purpose was to create in himself one new man out of the two, thus making peace, and in this one body to reconcile both of them to God through the cross, by which he put to death their hostility. He came and preached peace to you who were far away and peace to those who were near. For through him we both have access to the Father by one Spirit" (NIV).

Earlier in 1 Corinthians 6:17 Paul became more specific when He said, "But he who unites himself with the Lord is one with him in spirit" (NIV). The Authentic New Testament translation says, "But he who unites himself with the Master forms a single spirit." Feeding on the great mystery of the church will make you produce great acts as one man.

A great example is found in the Acts 3. There was a crippled man from birth that was laid at the entrance of the temple everyday. When Peter and John approached the temple at the hour of prayer, they noticed this man and spoke to him.

Acts 3:4-9 records, "And fixing his eyes on him, with John, Peter said, "Look at us." So he gave them his attention, expecting to receive something from them. Then Peter said, "Silver and gold I do not have, but what I do have I give you: In the name of Jesus Christ of Nazareth, rise up and walk." And he took him by the right hand and lifted him up, and immediately his feet and anklebones received strength. So he, leaping up, stood and walked and entered the temple with them — walking, leaping, and praising God."

Peter said, "Look at us." Somewhere in "rightly dividing the truth" of God's Word, we have lost our position as the deliverer of God's benefits and stand waiting for God to rescue us. Many would like to explain this passage by inferring that Peter had a gift of the spirit in operation, which made him so assertive and bold. This is very irrelevant when considering the position that Peter assumed.

Whether someone has a gift in operation or relies on the power of our redemption, the anointing works when we know we have it and believe we can release it at will. Peter took the responsibility of obtaining what was necessary to deliver this man. Peter said, "Look at us," not look at Jesus. We are so inclined to try to get all the attention off of us and onto Jesus that we overlook the fact that what we reveal of Jesus will be all the people will know.

Peter was not stealing the Lord's glory by drawing the attention to what was in his possession. When it comes time to use what we have been given by the Lord Jesus Christ, we must believe that we really have it to use. It is a sure fact that we possess nothing outside of what has been given from above. Peter could not heal this man without the assistance of the Holy Ghost. Every work of the supernatural is directly attributed to the *super* of God working through the natural of man! All glory is always given to the Lord Jesus!

The Supernatural
Every work of the supernatural is directly attributed to the *super* of God working through the natural of man! All glory is always given to the Lord Jesus!

Yet in operation, what we have been given must be used as though we possess it and have access to its benefits. Earlier we mentioned that Jesus never acted as though he was in a difficulty that merited more of God to rescue Him. Actually, only once did Jesus pray to the

Father for assistance, as seen before the working of the resurrection of Lazarus from the dead. As we will see from John 11:41-42, there was a good reason why Jesus prayed this prayer, "So they took away the stone. Then Jesus looked up and said, 'Father, I thank you that you have heard me. I knew that you always hear me, but I said this for the benefit of the people standing here, that they may believe that you sent me'" (NIV).

It is so important that a paradigm be shifted from believing God to do everything that will complete the mission of the Lord Jesus Christ, to our acceptance of the responsibility to initiate through our faith the plan and will of God in the earth.

Each individual must see himself or herself "in Christ," strengthened and empowered to accomplish each task. Never should there be a lull in our performance to wait on God.

- Could it be that He really waits on us?
- If this were true, then what would cause you and me to make a difference?

No one ever successfully preformed what they were destined to do, until they first accepted what God made them to be — a new creation in Christ.

As members of the body of Christ, you and I must continue to see ourselves in union with the Lord — one in purpose and ability to accomplish the destiny of the ages!

CHAPTER 7

RECOGNITION

When they had crossed over, they came to the land of Gennesaret. And when the men of that place ***recognized Him****, they sent out into all that surrounding region, brought to Him all who were sick, and begged Him that they might only touch the hem of His garment. And as many as touched it were made perfectly well.* (Matthew 14:34-36)

Recognition is the first step toward acknowledgment. Have you ever looked at someone familiar — someone you haven't seen in a long time — only to fail to recognize them? Perhaps their appearance has changed or their habits are different from what you had remembered. Recognition is wonderful...Webster calls it "special notice, or attention." Actions and proper responses are possible when we accurately recognize those we are looking for.

Jesus crossed over by boat to the land of Gennesaret. The men of Gennesaret recognized Jesus as the worker of miracles. They quickly went about the region to find all the sick they could, that they might bring them to Jesus for healing. Notice that the success ratio in this town was quite different from His own hometown. In Jesus' hometown of Nazareth, he was only able to heal a few that were sick.

> *Then He went out from there and came to His own country, and His disciples followed Him. And when the Sabbath had come, He began to teach in the synagogue. And many hearing Him were astonished, saying, "Where did this Man get these things? And what wisdom is this which is given to Him, that such mighty works are performed by His hands! Is this not the carpenter, the Son of Mary, and brother of James, Joses, Judas, and Simon? And are not His sisters here with us?" So they were offended at Him.*
>
> *But Jesus said to them, "A prophet is not without honor except in his own country, among his own relatives, and in his own house." Now He could do no mighty work there, except that He laid His hands on a few sick people and healed them. And He marveled because of their unbelief. Then He went about the villages in a circuit, teaching.* (Mark 6:1-7)

Wouldn't it have been more desirous for Jesus to heal in His own town, among His own people? If there were any place that would do your heart good to see people healed and delivered, wouldn't it be in your hometown among your relatives and close friends? It is always thrilling to have the approval of those you love. Yet, because of their unbelief, the majority of people were not helped. They were unable to receive anything. Jesus found that His hometown crowd was offended by Him. They would not believe that He was the Messiah, the Son of God.

In one sense, and because of their previous association with Jesus, we might be able to understand their unbelief. For they knew Him as the carpenter, they were even familiar with his whole family. They mentioned His brothers and sisters as a means of identification. Why was it so difficult for them to recognize the anointing on Jesus, especially when He told of many mighty miracles?

To His family and friends, Jesus was just a human being. Because of their familiarity to the natural man, they didn't honor the anointing. For that matter, they didn't believe that Jesus was "the anointed one."

Didn't Jesus Heal Everyone?

The gospels reveal a significant number of instances where Jesus was in the midst of a large crowd and only one person was recorded as being healed or helped. Why would this be? You might be thinking, "Didn't Jesus heal everyone?" Rightly dividing this thought is extremely important to our faith being strong in the Lord's commitment to us.

Jesus healed all who willingly approached Him in faith. However, He was unable to help those who rejected Him. Let's look at Mark 10:46-52, the story of blind Bartemaeus.

> *Now they came to Jericho. As He went out of Jericho with His disciples and a great multitude, blind Bartimaeus, the son of Timaeus, sat by the road begging. And when he heard that it was Jesus of Nazareth, he began to cry out and say, "Jesus, Son of David, have mercy on me!"*
>
> *Then many warned him to be quiet; but he cried out all the more, "Son of David, have mercy on me!"*
>
> *So Jesus stood still and commanded him to be called.*
>
> *Then they called the blind man, saying to him, "Be of good cheer. Rise, He is calling you."*
>
> *And throwing aside his garment, he rose and came to Jesus.*
>
> *So Jesus answered and said to him, "What do you want Me to do for you?"*
>
> *The blind man said to Him, "Rabboni, that I may receive my sight."*
>
> *Then Jesus said to him, "Go your way; your faith has made you well." And immediately he received his sight and followed Jesus on the road.*

It would seem from this passage that Bartimaeus recognized something about Jesus that no one else did. The Apostle Mark interprets the crowd as a great multitude. Let's say that there were a few thousand people following Jesus. This would make a great commotion. Bartimaeus was anxiously asking for information. What is the reason for the excitement among this great crowd of people? When he inquired about the noise, he was told that Jesus of Nazareth was passing by. Was this a correct statement? Yes, from the natural point of view, it was.

Jesus was a man from Nazareth. Now look at how Bartimaeus responds; "Son of David, have mercy on me." Bartimaeus didn't call Jesus as everyone else did. Consider also that no one else was healed in this crowd that we have record of. What was it that Bartimaeus knew about Jesus that everyone else didn't?

The name, "Son of David," is the covenant name for the fulfillment of the "sure mercies of David." God had prophesied to David that there would be one who would sit on his throne forever. The linage of David would produce an offspring who would be the Messiah. As a fulfillment of the covenant, God would grant mercy to every one who would believe and receive Him. Consequently, Bartimaeus cried out, "Son of David, have mercy on me." Even in the midst of the rejection of those standing around him, Bartimaeus cried out all the more.

To Bartimaeus the miraculous was guaranteed if only Jesus would hear his cry. When covenant is being fulfilled, there is no possible way of failure because recognition leads to faith. Bartimaeus not only recognized

CALLING ON HIS NAME

BARTIMAEUS NOT ONLY RECOGNIZED SOMETHING ABOUT JESUS THAT EVERYONE ELSE FAILED TO SEE, BUT HE ALSO ACTED IN FAITH BY CALLING ON JESUS AND OBEYING THE COMMAND OF FAITH THAT JESUS GAVE HIM.

something about Jesus that everyone else failed to see, but he also acted in faith by calling on Jesus and obeying the command of faith that Jesus gave him.

It is possible that others, at this point, were convinced that Jesus was more than the carpenter from Nazareth. But we don't have any other healings recorded at this particular place of ministry. We do know, however, that Bartimaeus respected and honored the anointing on the life of Jesus. Even though he was without sight, he could certainly believe the Scriptures that prophesied that the Messiah, Jesus, was the answer to all his problems.

Recognizing Jesus and Acting in Faith

Luke 5 has another intriguing story that will isolate an individual's faith from the crowd's unbelief.

> *Now it happened on a certain day, as He was teaching, that there were Pharisees and teachers of the law sitting by, who had come out of every town of Galilee, Judea, and Jerusalem. And the power of the Lord was present to heal them. Then behold, men brought on a bed a man who was paralyzed, whom they sought to bring in and lay before Him. 19 And when they could not find how they might bring him in, because of the crowd, they went up on the housetop and let him down with his bed through the tiling into the midst before Jesus.*
>
> *When He saw their faith, He said to him, "Man, your sins are forgiven you."*
>
> *And the scribes and the Pharisees began to reason,*

saying, "Who is this who speaks blasphemies? Who can forgive sins but God alone?"

But when Jesus perceived their thoughts, He answered and said to them, "Why are you reasoning in your hearts? Which is easier, to say, 'Your sins are forgiven you,' or to say, 'Rise up and walk'? But that you may know that the Son of Man has power on earth to forgive sins" — He said to the man who was paralyzed, "I say to you, arise, take up your bed, and go to your house."

Immediately he rose up before them, took up what he had been lying on, and departed to his own house, glorifying God. And they were all amazed, and they glorified God and were filled with fear, saying, "We have seen strange things today!" (Luke 5:17-27)

This story illustrates the importance of recognizing the anointing of God in the life of Jesus and then honoring it. Four friends gathered together — as an act of faith — to carry their friend to the meeting place where Jesus was speaking. Their intentions are obvious to see. They were confident that once their friend was in the presence of Jesus, he would receive the help he so desperately needed.

We could say that they recognized the significance of Jesus or perhaps just believed in Him as the miracle worker. We do know for certain that they didn't hesitate to act out their intentions. When opposition met them, they quickly overcame it.

The strength of their actions is seen in the power of their convictions. They believed so strongly that Jesus was the answer to their friend's problems that no matter what the obstacle, they would prevail. Even tearing off a roof was no obstacle — but became the solution.

Don't Give Up
Faith never gives up. To make a way where there seems to be no way is the bread and butter of faith! The absoluteness of God's Word will always silence the toughest storm.

Faith never gives up. To make a way where there seems to be no way is the bread and butter of faith! The absoluteness of God's Word will always silence the toughest storm.

If we look at this even further, we know that the power of God was present to heal all who were in the room. If the power of God was there to heal all, then we can assume that there was more than just one who had need of healing. God certainly knows. Again, there is only one recorded healing.

The room was primarily filled with Pharisees and Sadducees. However, if there were others present, they could easily have been heavily influenced by these religious leaders. The power of God was there to heal anyone who would openly receive it. The crippled man openly received it. He certainly made a notable entrance. This action of faith definitely warranted the response of Jesus. Very simply, this man had faith to get to Jesus. And everyone could see his faith in action.

Another important point to see is how Jesus coached the man to believe even as he still lay on the suspended cot. This is the reason why the man knew what to do to get his complete healing. Jesus moved this man to an action of faith to actually receive his healing. Yes, the man believed that Jesus was the answer, yet he lacked his own initiative to respond to the power of God. Jesus helped him at this point. It's wonderful to know that the simple recognition of spiritual things causes sensible actions of faith to follow.

Once there is a spiritual awareness, then there can be actions of faith. The reverse is also visible in this passage of Scripture. The power of the Lord was present, yet all those religious leaders failed to recognize it. Could the power of the Lord be recognizable to some and not to others?

For example, when you consider what Jesus talked about all the time, it's no wonder He had such sensitivity to the things of the Spirit. When you find Jesus in discussion with his disciples or the Pharisees, He is always talking about His Father, the anointing, and His mission. Spiritual things were constantly the thoughts and aspirations of Jesus. His life was lived doing the will of His Father. No doubt about it, the more you familiarize yourself with spiritual things, the easier it will be to access them.

The last example we have to illustrate this particular thought is the woman with the issue of blood found in Mark 5.

Now a certain woman had a flow of blood for twelve years, and had suffered many things from many physicians. She had spent all that she had and was no better, but rather grew worse. When she heard about Jesus, she came behind Him in the crowd and touched His garment. For she said, "If only I may touch His clothes, I shall be made well."

Immediately the fountain of her blood was dried up, and she felt in her body that she was healed of the affliction. And Jesus, immediately knowing in Himself that power had gone out of Him, turned around in the crowd and said, "Who touched My clothes?"

But His disciples said to Him, "You see the multitude thronging You, and You say, 'Who touched Me?'"

And He looked around to see her who had done this thing. But the woman, fearing and trembling, knowing what had happened to her, came and fell down before Him and told Him the whole truth. And He said to her, "Daughter, your faith has made you well. Go in peace, and be healed of your affliction."

(Mark 5:25-34)

Again, notice that a multitude of people was following Jesus. But only one healing is recorded. Let's find the reason. Once we find the particulars to this woman's case in verses 25-26, then we can see how she became involved with the ministry of Jesus.

First, she heard about Jesus. Of course, what she heard

had a tremendous influence on her actions. What if she had heard the wrong thing? She might not have responded at all to the opportunity. We can see what she heard by what she says. She heard that Jesus was anointed to heal all sickness and all disease with the power of God. Jesus Himself preached this message everywhere He went. Jesus would take the book of Isaiah and find the place where it was written, "the Spirit of the Lord is upon me, because He has anointed me." (Luke 4).

This woman believed that Jesus was anointed with something that would heal and set her free. She even believed that this power of God was upon Him to the degree that she could but touch His garment alone and receive the anointing. Therefore, she acted until she had fulfilled the faith that was in her heart.

It's not surprising at all to see the result of her faith. However, it is surprising to see the response of the disciples to Jesus when He asks, "Who touched me?" The whole multitude was thronging Jesus. This means that they were touching Him, trying to get close enough to see what was so special about Him. They certainly were not in faith like the woman who was healed because no one else received anything. After we understand this woman's perspective about Jesus, it's clear to see why she received her healing that day.

RECOGNITION
THE RECOGNITION OF SPIRITUAL THINGS IS THE BEGINNING OF THE ACTION OF FAITH.

Again, our point is also clear: *the recognition of spiritual things is the beginning of the action of faith.*

Jesus spent much time informing the disciples about His departure from the earth. We can read about this in John 14-16.

> *"If you love me, you will obey what I command. And I will ask the Father, and he will give you another Counselor to be with you forever- the Spirit of truth. The world cannot accept him, because it neither sees him nor knows him. But you know him, for he lives with you and will be in you. I will not leave you as orphans; I will come to you. Before long, the world will not see me anymore, but you will see me. Because I live, you also will live. On that day you will realize that I am in my Father, and you are in me, and I am in you. Whoever has my commands and obeys them, he is the one who loves me. He who loves me will be loved by my Father, and I too will love him and show myself to him."* (John 14:15-21 NIV)

Notice how Jesus prepares his disciples to recognize the new comforter, the Holy Ghost. He reveals the plan of the Father to abide in the heart of man. Jesus is telling them that the season whereby His presence has been abiding with them, naturally, will now be coming to an end. Since this is all that the disciples know and understand, up to this point, they will need much assurance that all will be the same or better after His departure. Remember, *without proper recognition, their faith will not act properly.*

Jesus declared, "You heard me say, 'I am going away and I am coming back to you.' If you loved me, you would be glad that I am going to the Father, for the Father is greater than I. I have told you now before it happens, so that when it does happen you will believe" (John 14:28-29 NIV)

God planned that there would be no difference having Jesus with Him, while the Holy Ghost is with us. Potentially, things will be even better as the presence of Jesus, that the disciples once enjoyed naturally, will come to abide in their hearts as a permanent awareness. Now more than ever, the disciples will be consciously aware of God and His power to overcome. So Jesus teaches, "When the Counselor comes, whom I will send to you from the Father, the Spirit of truth who goes out from the Father, he will testify about me. And you also must testify, for you have been with me from the beginning" (John 15:26-27 NIV).

Then in John 16 (NIV), Jesus further reveals what is to happen,

> *"Now I am going to him who sent me, yet none of you asks me, 'Where are you going?' Because I have said these things, you are filled with grief. But I tell you the truth: It is for your good that I am going away. Unless I go away, the Counselor will not come to you; but if I go, I will send him to you"* (verses 5-8).
>
> *"I have much more to say to you, more than you can now bear. But when he, the Spirit of truth, comes,*

he will guide you into all truth. He will not speak on his own; he will speak only what he hears, and he will tell you what is yet to come. He will bring glory to me by taking from what is mine and making it known to you. All that belongs to the Father is mine. That is why I said the Spirit will take from what is mine and make it known to you" (verses 12-15).

FEAR
FEAR BLOCKS OUR RECOGNITION OF GOD'S PRESENCE AND HINDERS FAITH.

"I have told you these things, so that in me you may have peace. In this world you will have trouble. But take heart! I have overcome the world" (verse 33).

Now Jesus knows that when He is gone, the most common emotion will be *fear*. Fear blocks our recognition of God's presence and hinders faith. So Jesus teaches His disciples in John's gospel to reject fear and embrace faith.

Put aside any spirit of fear. Act in faith. Recognize that the King of Kings, Jesus, is at your side—in the Holy Spirit.

It's time now to act. Stand firm in faith. Jesus wants us to **recognize** that through His presence, in the power of the Holy Spirit, we can have the same confidence and boldness that the disciples experienced. In fact, we can see His miraculous power manifested in a greater measure. Act in faith!

CHAPTER 8

Knowing God

"If you had known Me, you would have known My Father also; and from now on you know Him and have seen Him." (John 14:7)

Jesus had the most amazing job, He was sent to reveal the Father God because fallen humanity couldn't see Him naturally. John wrote in John 1:17-18, "No one has seen God at any time. The only begotten Son, who is in the bosom of the Father, He has declared Him."

To declare the Father is to make Him known or introduce Him. The beginning of the verse says that no one has seen God at any time. Even Phillip asked the question, Lord if you can show us the Father, then we'll believe? Jesus replied, "If you have seen me, you have seen the Father." God wants us to know Him. If in the natural, we were unable to see the Father, then how would it be possible to intimately know Him? It is true that to see the beauty in nature is to know that God exists, but what about knowing Him personally?

Faith is and has always been the key to the supernatural. Jesus manifested the anointing by faith and cultivated a relationship with the Father by faith. He led the way for anyone to follow.

Thirst and Hunger After God

God is pleased by our desire to know Him. When we are hungry and thirsty for God we will find Him. David had a passion for all of God he could obtain.

O God, You are my God;
Early will I seek You;
My soul thirsts for You;
My flesh longs for You
In a dry and thirsty land
Where there is no water.
So I have looked for You in the sanctuary,
To see Your power and Your glory.

Because Your lovingkindness is better than life,
My lips shall praise You.
Thus I will bless You while I live;
I will lift up my hands in Your name.
My soul shall be satisfied as with marrow and fatness,
And my mouth shall praise You with joyful lips.
(Psalm 63:1-5)

David understood that the first necessary element to finding God is *desire*. People without desire are people without purpose. Challenge yourself to see how important it is to succeed. In so many areas of natural life people will do anything to have the best.

- What would we do if knowing God were the primary way to become successful?
- Would this change your perspective about developing a relationship with God?

Certainly we serve God because we love and honor Him for all He means to us. We would be indebted forever if we were to pay for what the Lord has done for us. The debt, however, has been paid. God's desire is to have our devotion because we love Him.

Thus says the LORD:
"Let not the wise man glory in his wisdom,
Let not the mighty man glory in his might,
Nor let the rich man glory in his riches;
But let him who glories glory in this,
That he understands and knows Me,
That I am the LORD, exercising lovingkindness, judgment, and righteousness in the earth.
For in these I delight," says the LORD.

(Jeremiah 9:23-24)

If we were to listen to the world and its concept of success, we might be thrilled to have glory, riches and might. Yet to God, the prerequisites to fulfillment are understanding and knowing Him. It seems as if God is saying, that as much as wisdom, might, riches and glory are important to the frame of a human, they all stem from Him.

Where does God fit in? God is the center of the circle through which all the benefits of life evolve. Without Him all would be fleeting and insignificant. We must understand that the satisfaction of a man's soul is first and foremost found in the heart of God. Expression in the heart of man is only found when independence from all but God is established. Contentment is learning to be independent from all circumstances, and still maintaining the joy of the Lord.

CONTENTMENT
WE MUST UNDERSTAND THAT THE SATISFACTION OF A MAN'S SOUL IS FIRST AND FOREMOST FOUND IN THE HEART OF GOD. CONTENTMENT IS LEARNING TO BE INDEPENDENT FROM ALL CIRCUMSTANCES, AND STILL MAINTAINING THE JOY OF THE LORD.

Solomon was an individual who had the choice to ask for anything in the world. Look at Solomon's hunger and thirst for knowing God:

> *At Gibeon the LORD appeared to Solomon during the night in a dream, and God said, "Ask for whatever you want me to give you."*
>
> *Solomon answered, "You have shown great kindness to your servant, my father David, because he was faithful to you and righteous and upright in heart. You have continued this great kindness to him and have given him a son to sit on his throne this very day.*
>
> *"Now, O LORD my God, you have made your servant king in place of my father David. But I am only a little child and do not know how to carry out my*

duties. Your servant is here among the people you have chosen, a great people, too numerous to count or number. So give your servant a discerning heart to govern your people and to distinguish between right and wrong. For who is able to govern this great people of yours?"

The Lord was pleased that Solomon had asked for this. So God said to him, "Since you have asked for this and not for long life or wealth for yourself, nor have asked for the death of your enemies but for discernment in administering justice, I will do what you have asked. I will give you a wise and discerning heart, so that there will never have been anyone like you, nor will there ever be. Moreover, I will give you what you have not asked for — both riches and honor — so that in your lifetime you will have no equal among kings. And if you walk in my ways and obey my statutes and commands as David your father did, I will give you a long life." Then Solomon awoke-and he realized it had been a dream. (1 Kings 3:4-15 NIV)

As we see, Solomon asked for wisdom and a discerning heart. This is a very close example to the Scripture reference of Jeremiah 9:23-24. Knowing God is to be prosperous, mighty and wise. Having these benefits without knowing God is to lose perspective on the purpose of life.

Make God First!

If God is going to fit into the reality of our everyday lives, then we must seek Him first in all that we do and say. He alone is life's priority! Jesus helps us here to understand why it's so important to seek after God first, "But seek first the kingdom of God and His righteousness, and all these things shall be added to you" (Matthew 6:33).

Priorities
If God is going to fit into the reality of our everyday lives, then we must seek Him first in all that we do and say. He alone is life's priority!

How important is it to know God? Everything in life, as it should be, originates in God. To accomplish anything without the glory going to God is superficial and lacks purpose. If God could and does clothe the lilies of the fields without our help, then do you suppose He will do the same for us, if we honor Him first?

The reason why God blessed Abel's offering and not Cain's has to do with the attitude in which they gave it. Abel gave immediately when increase came. He blessed God with the firstfruits of his flocks. On the other hand, Cain gave God His portion when he got around to it. Knowing God has so much to do with our priorities!

If God is first in your life, then you will spend time with Him. Your day will evolve around your time with God. It's remarkable how God's principles work. If we'll sow time to God, we will reap plenty of time for ourselves.

Making God First Requires Faith

Jesus has the most wonderful relationship with the Father, which sets a standard for us to attain. Let's see how Jesus talks about His Father, "And He said to them, 'Why did you seek Me? Did you not know that I must be about My Father's business?' And Jesus increased in wisdom and stature, and in favor with God and men" (Luke 2:49,52).

As we can see, from Jesus' youth, He understood from His study of Scripture the destiny of His future. Jesus, at this young age, recognized the significance of developing a relationship with His Father. The necessary element for this relationship would be *faith*. Enoch used faith to contact God and then began a relationship with God that lasted 300 years on the earth.

Jesus touched the heart of His Father through His belief in the Father and His complete submission to the divine will of God. Then as we see Him in the gospels, we see how much He stayed in contact with the supernatural realm. Jesus constantly talked about His Father and the anointing:

> *"I tell you the truth, the Son can do nothing by himself; he can do only what he sees his Father doing, because whatever the Father does the Son also does. For the Father loves the Son and shows him all he does. Yes, to*

your amazement he will show him even greater things than these. (John 5:19-21 NIV)

"And the Father who sent me has himself testified concerning me. You have never heard his voice nor seen his form, nor does his word dwell in you, for you do not believe the one he sent." (John 5:37-39 NIV)

"Just as the living Father sent me and I live because of the Father, so the one who feeds on me will live because of me." (John 6:57)

"I am telling you what I have seen in the Father's presence, and you do what you have heard from your father." (John 8:38 NIV)

When you communicate your faith, God fits into everything in your life. Philemon 6 declares, "That the sharing of your faith may become effective by the acknowledgment of every good thing which is in you in Christ Jesus." In other words, the more you communicate and acknowledge the facts that exist in God, the more prone you are to walk in them.

SHARING FAITH

THE MORE JESUS SHARED ABOUT THE ANOINTING THAT WAS UPON HIM, THE EASIER IT WAS TO ACCESS IT AND RECOGNIZE IT. GREAT BENEFITS OBVIOUSLY FOLLOWED THE PEOPLE WHO WERE LISTENING TO JESUS, FOR THEY RECEIVED FAITH IN GOD FOR THE MIRACULOUS.

If Jesus always talked about His Father, His faith would then be strong concerning the realness of His Father's presence. The more Jesus shared about the anointing that was upon Him, the easier it was to access it and recognize it. Great benefits obviously followed the people who were listening to Jesus, for they received faith in God for the miraculous.

If we will remember, there is always a twofold work occurring when it comes to the manifestation of anything that is real in God. For instance, there is a dual force working in redemption. First, we know the truth of the reality of God. Jesus did die and rise again, to secure for the world complete freedom from the curse of sin. Before you received your redemption it was already a settled fact in the will of God. The provision was made two thousand years ago.

Second, the experience of this fact became reality when you confessed Jesus as Lord and Savior. Likewise, everything in redemption is a fact. Ephesians 1:3 declares, "Praise be to the God and Father of our Lord Jesus Christ, who has blessed us in the heavenly realms with every spiritual blessing in Christ" (NIV)

These benefits are real even though they may seem to have eluded you for the moment. If it were not given by God, then it couldn't be revealed by faith. Yet the fact is that all things that pertain to life and godliness have been given to us. Working out our salvation so that we can partake of it now is a job for faith. If something from God weren't real, then my confessions of faith and my actions of faith would be useless. However, what has already been conceived in God and provided for by Him will only be realized when we *act* in faith. This brings us to the development of our relationship with God.

Knowing the Shepherd

Jesus always spoke with absolutes. This made His ministry irresistible. People were never in doubt about what they were to expect. Since Jesus proved to the people, over and over again, that what He said would come to pass, their expectations were always high — a positive expectation. Even when Jesus spoke about the disciples and believers who would follow Him, He spoke with absolute truth.

All disciples and any followers of Jesus are classified as sheep. Jesus spoke about these sheep in John 10:2-5, "But he who enters by the door is the shepherd of the sheep. To him the doorkeeper opens, and the sheep hear his voice; and he calls his own sheep by name and leads them out. And when he brings out his own sheep, he goes before them; and the sheep follow him, for they know his voice. Yet they will by no means follow a stranger, but will flee from him, for they do not know the voice of strangers."

Notice how emphatically Jesus reveals the knowledge that the sheep have of their shepherd. Jesus said that His sheep hear His voice and are led by their shepherd. They follow Him because they know His voice. Then in contrast, Jesus went on to say, that His sheep do not know the voice of the stranger and they do not choose to follow him.

We have the choice to either believe Jesus or deny His words and confession of facts about us. Nowhere does Jesus say that we *will* know and hear Him. Knowing and hearing Jesus is not a future promise; it's a *now* reality! So, Jesus very clearly says that we *do* know Him and we *do* hear His voice. Again notice John 10:14, 27-29, "I am the good shepherd; and I know My sheep, and am known by My own. My sheep hear My voice, and I know them, and they follow Me. And I give them eternal life, and they shall never perish; neither shall anyone snatch them out of My hand."

Act in Faith

As sheep, how must we respond to Jesus' words? First, believe it and second, act like it's true. When we begin to talk as though we know the Lord and hear His voice, then we are acting in faith.

As sheep, how must we respond to Jesus' words? First, believe it and second, act like it's true. When we begin to talk as though we know the Lord and hear His voice, then we are acting in faith. We will never know the Lord unless knowing is preceded by faith. And we will never hear his voice until our faith tunes our listening. The action of faith must precede the experience.

If you continually want to know Him, then most likely you will always be wanting. The same is true for hearing His voice and following Him. When you accept the truth that you do know Him, then knowing Him becomes natural. You must also believe that you hear His voice before you ever have the experience of hearing the sound of His words in your heart.

Don't wait until you know how to follow Him, believe that you do follow Him before you know where to go. Anyone can hear Him if an audible voice is spoken, anyone can know Him when He makes Himself known, and it is easy to follow someone if you can see them. Yet these actions are walking by sight or by the physical senses.

Dare to break out of the box of tradition and religion. All religion and tradition is rooted in the senses. However, faith pleases God. The greatest honor to us and the most wonderful blessing to the Lord is that we forge a relationship with Him.

The application to this wonderful teaching of our Lord is to take each factual statement that Jesus made and respond to it as though it is real right now. Any time we fail to respond to the Word of God, we actually accuse God of lying. God wouldn't say that you know Him if you didn't.

Begin to say, "Father, it's so good to know You. I'm so glad to understand and comprehend Your ways. Regardless of the circumstances that come, I know what to do, because I hear Your voice."

It is amazing to see what happens when we yield our thoughts and actions to the Word of God.

James writes about this same type of faith in action. "If any of you lacks wisdom, let him ask of God, who gives to all liberally and without reproach, and it will be given to him. But let him ask in faith, with no doubting, for he who doubts is like a wave of the sea driven and tossed by the wind. For let not that man suppose that he will receive anything from the Lord; he is a double-minded man, unstable in all his ways" (James 1:5-8).

James makes it very clear in the fifth verse that God is a *giver* when we pray. If you ask God for something that His Word promises, you can be sure that He will give or supply you with the answer. In the case of wisdom, why would verse five reiterate the fact that God will give you wisdom? The fact that God will give is mentioned twice. The reason for this is found in verse six. James starts out by saying, "but let him ask in faith."

Wisdom Waits

OF COURSE, ONCE YOU HAVE ACCEPTED THE WISDOM OF GOD BY FAITH, YOU CAN'T BE ANXIOUS ABOUT WHAT TO DO. IT'S ALSO PATIENTLY BELIEVING IN YOUR HEART SO THAT EVERYTHING YOU DO IS INFLUENCED BY WHAT YOU HAVE RECEIVED BY FAITH.

If God gives you wisdom, how do you know you have it? When you know what to do? Have we reached the same dilemma? If receiving from God is only when we have the physical evidence of what we have believed for, then we wouldn't be using faith. James reminds us that faith is going to be the key to experiencing the wisdom.

Regardless of what your mind seems to comprehend the moment you ask, you would respond as if you already have the wisdom you need. You might pray," Lord, thank you for giving me the wisdom that I need. You know how important it is that I know and understand completely what to do. Thank you, Lord, everything will be just perfect now."

Of course, once you have accepted the wisdom of God by faith, you can't be anxious about what to do. Receiving what you need from God is not just saying the right thing like a password that opens the door. It is also patiently believing in your heart so that everything you do is influenced by what you have received by faith.

Concerning the topic of "knowing God," isn't it wonderful to *know* Him—Jesus said we do. So you might as well count on it, because you do know Him!

The Spirit Helps Us Know God

There is one more thought that will complete this study on knowing God. Jesus said that we have been given a Helper in every area of life. Jesus promised, "And I will pray the Father, and He will give you another Helper, that He may abide with you forever — the Spirit of truth, whom the world cannot receive, because it neither sees Him nor knows Him; but you know Him, for He dwells with you and will be in you" (John 14:16-17).

The Holy Spirit is the Helper sent from the Father to live with us and in us, to make all of life successful. The Holy Spirit is the anointing that comes to abide with us. Jesus accomplished His mission on the earth because the Holy Spirit empowered Him to succeed.

The Holy Spirit will always lead us in accordance with the Word. As Jesus submitted Himself to the will of the Father, the Holy Spirit worked in Him to produce evidence that Jesus knew God.

You can always count on the work of the Holy Spirit as long as you stay true to God's Word. Jesus said that the Holy Ghost would reveal the heart and will of the Father. Jesus declared, "However, when He, the Spirit of truth, has come, He will guide you into all truth; for He will not speak on His own authority, but whatever He hears He will speak; and He will tell you things to come. He will glorify Me, for He will take of what is Mine and declare it to you. All things that the Father has are Mine. Therefore I said that He will take of Mine and declare it to you" (John 16:13-15).

Isn't this awesome? While we are actively working with the Word and becoming increasingly aware of our knowledge of God, the Holy Ghost is working with the same goal in mind: *to reveal to us the Lord and our Father.* It is our faith that works with God and the revelation of the Holy Ghost that works with us to produce the finished product of knowing God, "But you have an anointing from the Holy One and you know all things" (1 John 2:20).

Notice how closely related the anointing and the knowledge of God are. Again look at what John wrote in 1 John 2:27, "But the anointing which you have received from Him abides in you, and you do not need that anyone teach you; but as the same anointing teaches you concerning all things, and is true, and is not a lie, and just as it has taught you, you will abide in Him."

The Holy Ghost will actually teach us how to abide in Him. God in His goodness gives us so many advantages in our relationship with Him.

- Jesus' declarations of truth, that we know God, give us the highest confidence and assurance for developing a knowledge of God.
- Then we have the inner working of the Holy Ghost to reveal the heart of God and teach us how to abide in Him.

Know God and Do Great Exploits!

Is there really any excuse for not knowing God? As Daniel said in 11:32, "The people who **know their God** shall be strong, and carry out great exploits." Knowing God, seeing God, hearing God, and following God become for us the tools of constant success.

Never was a believer successful who didn't know God. To complete the will of God without knowing God would be impossible. Every area of your life hinges on your relationship with God. Working with the Teacher (the Holy Spirit) and being constantly aware of His indwelling presence is to be the securest of believers.

When we *know God,* we understand *how, when and where God fits in* for every situation and relationship in our lives.

Knowing God

- transforms confusion into clarity.
- moves us from operating in just the natural to doing mighty, supernatural exploits.
- gives us the assurance to act in faith.
- frees us from anxiety and fear and releases us into bold courage.

KNOWING GOD

KNOWING GOD TRANSFORMS CONFUSION INTO CLARITY.

KNOWING GOD MOVES US FROM OPERATING IN JUST THE NATURAL TO DOING MIGHTY, SUPERNATURAL EXPLOITS.

Join me in applying these truths we've just learned to your life. God has made it so easy for us. Why wouldn't we desire to dive right in and experience God? I'm continually amazed at the simplicity of God's profound truths. God has done everything to help us to walk in constant success. Nothing less than this is acceptable to Him. If we will be honest with ourselves, should anything else be acceptable to us either?

CHAPTER 9

Abiding in Him

If you abide in Me, and My words abide in you, you will ask what you desire, and it shall be done for you. By this My Father is glorified, that you bear much fruit; so you will be My disciples. (John 15:7-8)

As profound as we like to be with our secrets of success, Jesus' instructions can be simply summarized: *read the Bible and pray.* Here is a Scripture that typifies the life and ministry of our Lord. John 3:13 says, "No one has ascended to heaven but He who came down from heaven, that is, the Son of Man who is in heaven." It is quite clear by the reading of this verse that Jesus maintained access to two worlds at the same time. While He was walking on this earth in the flesh, He was living out of Heaven through His contact with the Spirit.

We know that Jesus prized His time spent with the Father and the Word of God more than food or rest. After a multitude of people was ministered to, Jesus retreated to a mountain alone to pray, just to meet another crowd the next day. It was His custom to rise early before the others to spend time alone in prayer. When questioned about His need for food, He commented to His disciples that, "man shall not live by bread alone, but by every word that proceeded out of the mouth of God." This great appetite displayed in the life of our Lord certainly demonstrates the commitment possible for those who are sold out to the will of God. Let's take a look at the word *abide,* and at least we'll have a good understanding of the commitment necessary for making progress in God.

Abiding Fits God into Everything in Life

The word *abide* is used to preface the reading of the Word and prayer. *Abide* means to remain and continue. This meaning would be equivalent to: "to not depart, not to leave, to continue to be present." This chapter is devoted to expressing God's view about abiding.

To God, *abiding* in the Word looks like this: "Do not let this Book of the Law depart from your mouth; meditate on it day and night, so that you may be careful to do everything written in it. Then you will be prosperous and successful." (Joshua 1:8 NIV)

If we take this literally, we would become extremely saturated with God's thoughts. Meditating day and night would not leave much time for carnality. Keeping the Word of God always on your tongue would certainly change the content of our conversations.

If you will notice, everything God tells us to do when it comes to the mind always ends up in some type of action. God loves development and growth. He is constantly preparing us to succeed by reshaping our thinking. When we step out to do the Word, after meditating day and night, there is a promise that you will be prosperous and successful. The end result, of course, sounds good, but what about the discipline necessary to change your paradigm?

Solomon wrote under the inspiration of the Holy Ghost that abiding in the Word looks like this:

> *My son, pay attention to what I say;*
> *listen closely to my words.*
> *Do not let them out of your sight,*
> *keep them within your heart;*
> *for they are life to those who find them*
> *and health to a man's whole body.*
> *Above all else, guard your heart,*
> *for it is the wellspring of life.*
> (Proverbs 4:20-23 NIV)

Renewed Thinking
God loves development and growth. He is constantly preparing us to succeed by reshaping our thinking.

As we can see in both passages of Scripture, continuing and remaining in the Word of God is required. The attention that we give anything will always influence the outcome of our experiences. What we embrace and act on will be seen tomorrow. Solomon, one of the wisest men that ever lived, said that we must give our attention to the Word. I remember years ago for a brief season I filled in as a substitute classroom teacher.

I learned that it was important to get the attention of the students before what I said would do any good.

The world is full of distractions. Focusing our attention on the Word takes effort. Paul said in Colossians 3:2, we are to set our minds on things that are above. In other words, our minds do not automatically go there.

It takes a conscious effort to keep your mind focused. Did you ever wonder what Paul meant when He said in Hebrews 4 that we are to labor to enter into the rest of the Lord? How then could faith be a work and a rest at the same time? The labor is the renewing of the mind; the rest is the entering into the peace that comes when you know that you know that God is at work. Faith is always inspired. When your mind is renewed, it's easy to get excited about what you believe. The rest comes when you know that you have the answer.

Reflecting back on our school experiences, and to grasp the concepts of what was taught, the word *repetition* is very familiar. Remember what it was like to study for an exam. Even though our teacher explained well the material in the classroom, we would study for hours the same material — over and over again. Our success had to do with how well we could recall the material. The more familiar we were with it, the easier the examination. It was not a good feeling to take the exam knowing that you were not as familiar with the material as you should be.

If we were to draw a parallel to the success of believers during their test of faith, we could see the same benefits to knowing well the answers to the test. Let me add; it is one thing to know the correct answers to the material, and an entirely different thing to live by the answers we know.

In Luke 4 Jesus passed a great test. We know from the Scriptures that Jesus was indeed a student of the Word. Luke 2:40 says, "And the Child grew and became strong in spirit, filled with wisdom; and the grace of God was upon Him." And verse 52 says, "And Jesus increased in wisdom and stature and in favor with God and men." When Jesus came to His hometown, He would stand up and read, "And He [Jesus] was handed the book of the prophet Isaiah. And when He had opened the book, He found the place where it was written."(Luke 4:17).

You cannot find something without looking for it. Even Jesus said, everyone who seeks will find. Jesus spent much time searching the Scriptures for information concerning who He was and what He was to do. Luke 4:1-13 (NIV) shows us that Jesus knew His material well.

> *Jesus, full of the Holy Spirit, returned from the Jordan and was led by the Spirit in the desert, where for forty days he was tempted by the devil. He ate nothing during those days, and at the end of them he was hungry.*

The devil said to him, "If you are the Son of God, tell this stone to become bread."

Jesus answered, "It is written: 'Man does not live on bread alone.'"

The devil led him up to a high place and showed him in an instant all the kingdoms of the world. And he said to him, "I will give you all their authority and splendor, for it has been given to me, and I can give it to anyone I want to. So if you worship me, it will all be yours."

Jesus answered, "It is written: 'Worship the Lord your God and serve him only.'"

The devil led him to Jerusalem and had him stand on the highest point of the temple. "If you are the Son of God," he said, "throw yourself down from here. For it is written: "'He will command his angels concerning you to guard you carefully; they will lift you up in their hands, so that you will not strike your foot against a stone.'"

Jesus answered, "It says: 'Do not put the Lord your God to the test.'" When the devil had finished all this tempting, he left him until an opportune time.

Jesus scored an A+ or one hundred per cent on His exam. Do you think His success had to do with how well the Word abode in Him? In order to be an effective doer of the Word, the Word has to abide in you. David was quoted as saying in Psalm 119 that the Word "have I hid in my heart, that I might not sin against thee." If the Word hid in your heart would keep you from sin, then the Word hid in your heart will produce blessings in your Christian walk. In other words, you need to spend time in the Word.

The Apostle Paul ran into some new converts in Berea that diligently sought to allow the Word of God to abide in them. Acts 17:11 says, "These were more fair-minded than those in Thessalonica, in that they received the word with all readiness, and searched the Scriptures daily to find out whether these things were so." Paul admonishes these because of their zealousness to search in the word for answers. This frame of mind displayed through the believers in Berea is almost a lost art in today's Christian mindset. There are far too many people that believe what they believe because Brother or Sister so and so said so.

In the Acts of the Apostles you could be bruised and take a good beating that way. Remember the Jewish exorcist? They tried to cast out a devil in the name of Jesus whom Paul preached. The devil commented, that he knew Paul and Jesus, although, these exorcists he did not know. They wound up beaten and naked. Does this sound much like the method of exorcism that Jesus demonstrated? He simply said, "Shut up and come out."

It is interesting that devils know you when you know who you are in the Lord. I believe it is very necessary to understand for ourselves the doctrine we preach.

James in his letter to the church had much to say about doing the Word.

> *Therefore putting aside all filthiness and all that remains of wickedness, in humility receive the word implanted, which is able to save your souls. But prove yourselves doers of the word, and not merely hearers who delude themselves. For if anyone is a hearer of the word and not a doer, he is like a man who looks at his natural face in a mirror; for once he has looked at himself and gone away, he has immediately forgotten what kind of person he was. But one who looks intently at the perfect law, the law of liberty, and abides by it, not having become a forgetful hearer but an effectual doer, this man shall be blessed in what he does.*
>
> (James 1:21-25 NAS)

Abiding in the Word of God is the most effective way to save your soul. The washing of the Word will cleanse your mind from the impurities of the world. Whether or not you know it, your mind has been brainwashed in the world's system of doubt and unbelief. Depending on how well immersed you are in skepticism will definitely determine the amount of Word it will take to cleanse your mind.

PURITY
THE WASHING OF THE WORD WILL CLEANSE YOUR MIND FROM THE IMPURITIES OF THE WORLD.

God Fits In When You Act in Faith!

Again, let me remind you that knowing the correct answers to life's problems is only the first step. The next step is when you are willing to act on what you believe. Faith is always inspired. When the Word of God is the only thing that makes sense to you, you are in a good place.

James said that the key to the Word working in your life is to act on it when you hear it. When Jesus taught the parable of the sower, there were four kinds of soil. The good soil related to those people who heard the Word with the intention of doing something with it. Until you hear the Word and act on it, the Word you hear will not be yours.

You would assume, then, that many people are self-deceived. The Word of God is only yours when you make a decision to act on it. Acting on the Word of God is always easier when you get excited about it.

Next, James draws the parallel of a man who looks at himself in a mirror; when he fails to act on the Word it is the same as going away and forgetting what you looked like in the mirror. Can you see the powerful truth intrinsic in the Word? It has the divine ability to produce an image in you. Abiding in the Word, to God, is a man who sees his reflection in the Word of God as God sees him. We are told in 2 Corinthians 4:3-4, "And even if our gospel is veiled, it is veiled to those who are perishing. The god of this age has blinded the minds of unbelievers, so that they cannot see the light of the gospel of the glory of Christ, who is the image of God" (NIV).

If Satan blinds the eyes of unbelievers, how much more will he endeavor to keep us as believers in the dark concerning the privileges, rights and dominion we have in Christ? Yes, the light has come to the redeemed of God! However, the learning curve is always on scale for continued development and growth. Abiding in the Word will insure that every area of our lives is blessed and prosperous.

The blessed person is the one who continues in the Word. As Moses said in Deuteronomy 4:9, "Only take heed to yourself, and diligently keep yourself, lest you forget the things your eyes have seen, and lest they depart from your heart all the days of your life. And teach them to your children and your grandchildren." If you want the Word to remain in your heart, you have to keep the Word of God before your eyes. By doing so, you will not be a forgetful hearer.

As you can see, abiding in the Word is spending time and allowing the Word to change your identity on the inside. Abiding in the Word is seeing yourself as God sees you.

How Do We Abide?

Application to abiding in the Word is really a simple process. The power of the Word is produced in the image it creates. God has given each of us an imagination. With the imagination, we can see on the inside. This is where understanding becomes more than information. Every believer is filled with faith; the nature and ability of God to believe just like Him. The potential of every born again believer to appropriate the blessings of God lies inherent within the nature of God.

Revelation is the inspiration to a man or woman's faith that spawns action. When you hear the Word or read it, the Holy Spirit is the one who causes excitement to fill your heart. Protect yourself against reading the Word of God in a dry, dead and boring way. Don't wait on God to make you do or feel something. That is not His job. Read and hear the Word of God in faith believing.

Approach the Word as if it's the first time you have ever read it. Be expectant that what you hear, you will comprehend. Look forward to using the Word in your every day life. When you are excited, the Holy Spirit will quicken truth to your heart. The Word will form an image. When you hear words, you actually hear them by seeing images.

Expectancy
APPROACH THE WORD AS IF IT'S THE FIRST TIME YOU HAVE EVER READ IT. BE EXPECTANT THAT WHAT YOU HEAR, YOU WILL COMPREHEND.

It is God's desire for you to see Him as He really is. He also wants you to see yourself as He sees you. God never made a failure. When you meditate, or mutter, speak and rehearse the Word of God, allow yourself to behold the image that the Word is creating. Since God created the worlds with His Word, then He can create in you through words an image that will become just as real as the earth He created.

The Word of God is a dynamic force whereby all your wildest imaginations are exceeded! If you should happen to get excited in the realities of God, you might just lose your perspective as to the failures and hardships of this carnal world. Thinking like this will get you bold and confident actions of faith. You do know what comes next, don't you? The material realm will give way to the greater realm of the Spirit, and what God says will be seen!

To Abide is To Avoid Distractions

If you will recall, Jesus said in the text of John 15:7 that we are also to abide in Him. What does it look like to God when we abide in Him? Luke 10:38-40 is a great passage of Scripture that shows us what it means to abide in Him: "As Jesus and his disciples were on their way, he came to a village where a woman named Martha opened her home to him. She had a sister called Mary, who sat at the Lord's feet listening to what he said. But Martha was distracted by all the preparations that had to be made. She came to him and asked, 'Lord, don't you care that my sister has left me to do the work by myself? Tell her to help me!'" (NIV)

Here are two sisters who chose to respond differently to the Lord. Mary's attention was given to the Lord, spending time at His feet. Not only was she attentive to be with the Lord, she was listening to what He said. On the other hand, Martha was too busy in natural things to give her attention to the Lord. As the Word says, she was distracted by all the preparations.

This demonstrates what we learned earlier; we each have a responsibility to keep our thoughts on the Word, and to give our attention directly to the Lord. Martha was distracted; on the other hand, Mary was focused.

When we consider the phrase, "abiding in Him," we must remember this to mean, "staying continually aware of and in connection with God." I can remember great men of God saying, if you can hold the devil in the faith realm, you can whip him every time. However, if he can hold you in the realm of reason, he will whip you every time. To me, it would look as if the realm you are more familiar with will get your greatest attention.

Let's look at another time when Martha and Mary were mentioned together. In John chapter 11 is the story of the brother of Martha and Mary named, Lazarus. He was sick unto death, when Jesus was given the information.

> *On his arrival, Jesus found that Lazarus had already been in the tomb for four days. Bethany was less than two miles from Jerusalem, and many Jews had come to Martha and Mary to comfort them in the loss of their brother. When Martha heard that Jesus was coming, she went out to meet him, but Mary stayed at home.*
>
> *"Lord," Martha said to Jesus, "if you had been here, my brother would not have died. But I know that even now God will give you whatever you ask." Jesus said to*

her, "Your brother will rise again." Martha answered, "I know he will rise again in the resurrection at the last day."

Jesus said to her, "I am the resurrection and the life. He who believes in me will live, even though he dies; and whoever lives and believes in me will never die. Do you believe this?"

"Yes, Lord," she told him, "I believe that you are the Christ, the Son of God, who was to come into the world." And after she had said this, she went back and called her sister Mary aside. "The Teacher is here," she said, "and is asking for you." When Mary heard this, she got up quickly and went to him. Now Jesus had not yet entered the village, but was still at the place where Martha had met him. When the Jews who had been with Mary in the house, comforting her, noticed how quickly she got up and went out, they followed her, supposing she was going to the tomb to mourn there.

When Mary reached the place where Jesus was and saw him, she fell at his feet and said, "Lord, if you had been here, my brother would not have died."

When Jesus saw her weeping, and the Jews who had come along with her also weeping, he was deeply moved in spirit and troubled. "Where have you laid him?" he asked.

"Come and see, Lord," they replied.

Jesus wept.

Then the Jews said, "See how he loved him!"

But some of them said, "Could not he who opened the eyes of the blind man have kept this man from dying?" Jesus, once more deeply moved, came to the tomb. It was a cave with a stone laid across the entrance. "Take away the stone," he said.

"But, Lord," said Martha, the sister of the dead man, "by this time there is a bad odor, for he has been there four days."

Then Jesus said, "Did I not tell you that if you believed, you would see the glory of God?"

So they took away the stone. Then Jesus looked up and said, "Father, I thank you that you have heard me. I knew that you always hear me, but I said this for the benefit of the people standing here, that they may believe that you sent me."

When he had said this, Jesus called in a loud voice, "Lazarus, come out!" The dead man came out, his hands and feet wrapped with strips of linen, and a cloth around his face.

Jesus said to them, "Take off the grave clothes and let him go" (NIV).

In verse 21, Martha meets up with Jesus and states her respect for Jesus by saying, that if Jesus had been here before Lazarus died, he never would have died. In the next verse, Martha surprises us by saying, "I know that whatever you ask of the Father, it will be yours." It looks from afar that this kind of revelation is what Jesus will use to springboard into the miracle of raising the dead. Jesus then responds, "Your brother will rise."

Martha, still thinking that she has a place in this conversation, says, "I know that in the resurrection he will rise." She just missed what Jesus was about to do. So now Jesus tells her, "I am the resurrection and the life. If you believe in me, you will live." And now Jesus asks her His first question, "Do you believe this?"

I do not believe Jesus is trying to make Martha look bad. After all, He is there to raise her brother. However, Jesus does have her located. She responds, "I believe that you are the Christ, the Son of God." This is a wonderful thing to believe; yet, it is not what Jesus asked of her. Can you see how we limit God? **When you cannot conceptualize the possibility of God's intervention, you limit Him.**

I wonder if Martha's familiarity to the natural had something to do with her lack of trust. It is not that Martha didn't have a good doctrine. It's just that when it came time to use it, it was not real to her.

On the other hand, in verse 32 when Mary came to the Lord for the first time, only her initial response was the same. To me this indicates that everyone was talking about how the Lord could have kept Lazarus from dying had He been there in time. I thank God that He is always on time, even if we feel He is not. After Mary spoke the same words of her sister, you do not see her speak again.

I wonder if her resolve was a result of her faith and trust that Jesus would remedy the situation. Even when Jesus commanded the stone to be removed, it wasn't Mary who spoke. It was Martha who reminded the Lord that after four days, the body would be decaying. Again, she was using natural thinking. Isn't it possible that the time that Mary spent with the Lord broadened her horizons to the possibilities of God? Could it be that she had become familiar enough to Jesus that she needed not to interfere? Oh that we would get our problems into the hands of God where the solutions are sure!

Abiding Reflects God's Glory

Abiding in Him has always been the desire of God for all who would make the effort to seek Him with all their heart. Moses was another who turned from his way of life to seek the Lord. Moses saw the burning bush that was not consumed; the Lord spoke when Moses turned to see the bush. You have to turn from those things that are distracting you before you will receive proper instructions from the Lord.

The Lord commanded Moses to deliver the people of God from Egyptian bondage. When it was time to free the children of God from Egypt, Moses was instructed to journey across the desert to the promised land. Two things had become dear to Moses throughout his training as God's man to deliver the children of God. One would be the Word of the Lord that continued to direct and instruct Moses in the ways of God. Second, would be Moses' familiarity with the glory of God, which in all situations would release the utmost confidence in God.

Moses always kept in mind his relationship with God. Exodus 33:7-11 reads,

> *Now Moses used to take a tent and pitch it outside the camp some distance away, calling it the "tent of meeting." Anyone inquiring of the LORD would go to the tent of meeting outside the camp. And whenever Moses went out to the tent, all the people rose and stood at the entrances to their tents, watching Moses until he entered the tent. As Moses went into the tent, the pillar of cloud would come down and stay at the entrance, while the LORD spoke with Moses. Whenever the people saw the pillar of cloud standing at the entrance to the tent, they all stood and worshiped, each at the entrance to his tent. The LORD would speak to Moses face to face, as a man speaks with his friend. Then Moses would return to the camp, but his young aide Joshua son of Nun did not leave the tent"* (NIV).

Notice how Moses pitched his tent outside the camp. The tent was some distance away from the camp. The camp represented what was familiar to Moses and the people. Removing yourself from what is familiar is the beginning of quality time with the Lord. Remember with me that the tent was called the "tent of meeting." How appropriate. It was a place where God and Moses would fellowship one with another.

We read in Numbers 12:3 that Moses was considered the meekest of men on the earth. This simply means that there was no one who depended upon the Lord like Moses. He learned to depend completely on God. Spending time in the glory will convince even the most rebellious in nature of the superiority and mightiness of God.

Moses had many wonderful experiences in the presence of God. To Moses, spending time in the glory of God was normal. The "tent of meeting" is uniquely named for the presence of God being manifested. The cloud of glory would hover over the tent, in expectation that Moses would come and fellowship with God.

Moses' young apprentice, Joshua, would linger in the presence of God. He learned how important it is to abide in the Lord. Staying in His presence will endear your heart to God Himself.

It is wonderful to know about God; yet how much better it is to spend time with Him! There is always a mark on the lives of people who know God from intimate time with Him. Moses spent enough time with God on the mountain, as he was receiving the Ten Commandments, that he actually began to glow with the glory of the Lord. This is an amazing thought. It can be likened to the Walt Disney movie, Peter Pan; there was a residue that followed the character Tinker Bell wherever she went. The residue was called pixie dust.

God's residue is called glory. *Cabod* is the Hebrew word for glory. Its meaning speaks of a weight, a heaviness or covering of iridescent splendor. If an individual were to stay in the presence of God for a good amount of time, his countenance would be covered with the glow of God's glory. Abiding in His presence produces blessing and peace in our lives.

> *And the LORD spoke to Moses, saying: "Speak to Aaron and his sons, saying, 'This is the way you shall bless the children of Israel. Say to them:*
>
> *"The LORD bless you and keep you;*
> *The LORD make His face shine upon you,*
> *And be gracious to you;*
> *The LORD lift up His countenance upon you,*
> *And give you peace."'*
> (Numbers 6:22-26)
>
> *There are many who say,*
> *"Who will show us any good?"*
> *LORD, lift up the light of Your countenance upon us.*
> (Psalm 4:6)

Blessing
Abiding in His presence produces blessing and peace in our lives.

These verses of Scripture reveal that God's presence can be detected. The more time you spend with God in your private time, the easier it will be to respond to what would please Him in every trial or situation.

The Apostle Paul commented in Romans 12:11 that we should not be "lagging in diligence, fervent in spirit, serving the Lord." Another translation says of this verse, "concerning being fervent in spirit that we are to maintain the glow." Glow is a shortened form of glory. We are to maintain the glory or stay in the presence of God until it is natural to act like God.

In the cartoon series, *Peanuts,* with the familiar characters of Charlie Brown, Lucy and Linus, there was a character called Pigpen. He always was seen with a cloud of dust following him around. His character was depicted by a countenance of messy things. Naturally speaking, we can often tell what a person is like by the attitude they have. Likewise, it is no secret that we as Christians are to be different from the world.

Can the world tell that we are different by the way we behave in public? Recently I had a car salesman, and friend, share with me a testimony after purchasing a new car from the dealership. He said that no one in his department liked to wait on the Christian customers who came to buy cars because of their attitudes. Some of their worst customers were the preachers, they were so demanding, and acted as if they ought to have something for free, so much so that the salesmen, both the saved ones and unsaved, tried to avoid waiting on them.

My friend commented that he wanted to thank me for the way I conducted myself. He said that it definitely gave a good testimony on two counts — being saved and being a preacher. I asked him what I did that made the difference. He simply stated that everything I did was with integrity and without contention. My response was that I wanted a car and I knew that he was doing everything he could to accommodate me.

I expected to pay money, so it wasn't a surprise when he quoted me a price. It makes me wonder whether Christians are expecting their blessing from the wrong source? When you can sow a car to bless someone, then you can expect to be blessed.

So then the "tent of meeting" that Moses entered, in order to spend time with God, was a place free of distractions. Moreover, it was Joshua who lingered in the glory after Moses left the tent. If a mountain can melt like wax at the presence of the Lord then surely a human being would be affected by spending time with God. In fact, it was Joshua and Caleb who were the only two spies out of twelve that had a good report about the promised land.

Moses was instructed to send twelve spies to check things out when the children of Israel came to the Jordan River. For forty days, the twelve spied the land before coming back with a report. Numbers chapter 13 records that ten spies gave an evil report before Moses and the children of Israel, which produced fear and unbelief. Only Joshua and Caleb returned with the report that God would give them the land. When you spend time with God, you will be strong and courageous.

There has never been anyone who focused more on the Word of God and on spending time in His presence like the Lord Jesus Christ did. Just as we have seen with Mary, her intentions were to give much time to being at the feet of Jesus. Even so, Jesus kept His focus both day and night on His Father.

What happens when we abide? We spend time with Jesus. We begin to reflect His presence and glory in our lives as we become like Him. When free from distractions, abiding in Him gives us the ability to see and know in every circumstance and relationship of life, where God fits in.

Take the guesswork out of life. Move from the natural into the supernatural. Develop a "tent of meeting" in your daily schedule. Come out of the familiar and step into His presence through His Word, through prayer, and being still before God. When you fit God into all that you do and say in your daily walk; when you abide, God will fit into your life in such a way that all you are will reflect His glory!

> *But we all, with unveiled face, beholding as in a mirror the glory of the Lord, are being transformed into the same image from glory to glory, just as by the Spirit of the Lord.* (2 Corinthians 3:18)

EPILOGUE

It's Your *Now* Moment

Now it's time to recognize His Presence.

Now it's time to abide in Christ.

Now it's time to begin living supernaturally.

Stop making excuses.

Refuse to squeeze God out of your every thought, feeling or action.

Let go of past habits that make you too busy to see God everywhere.

Pray, *now.*

Act in faith, *now.*

Take God at His Word, *now.*

Don't procrastinate.

Eliminate doubts.

Discard life's negatives for God's promises.

God will never fit in your life until you totally surrender and fit into the life of God.

Why resist? Why not surrender?

Now is the moment for God to fit in for you in every thought, feeling, action and decision. Get beyond asking, "Where does God fit in?" Begin confessing, "God fits in all things, at all times, in all ways, for all good and all blessing in my life!"

Make Romans 8:28-32, your faith confession *now:*

I know that in all things God works for my good for I love him and have been called according to his purpose. For God foreknew me and also predestined me to be conformed to the likeness of his Son, that he might be the firstborn among many brothers. And having predestined me, God also called me; having called me, he also justified me; having justified me, he also glorified me.

How then shall I respond to this? If God is for me, who can be against me? Hallelujah! Amen.

(adapted from NIV)

About the Author

Jim Hockaday was raised in a Christian home where he was born again at four years of age. He experienced the call of God on his life and the desire to preach even in these early years.

After graduating from Wheaton College in 1983, he traveled and ministered with several Christian music groups, including the Spurlows, Truth, and the Living Word Singers.

When God put in Jim's heart a strong desire to know more of Him, he attended Rhema Bible Training Center and graduated in 1988. Immediately following graduation, he joined the Rhema Singers and Band and traveled extensively with Rev. Kenneth E. Hagin and the group for nearly seven years.

Since 1994, Jim has been the coordinator of Prayer and Healing School for Kenneth Hagin Ministries of Broken Arrow, OK, ministering daily in both Prayer School and Healing School. It has been Jim's heart's desire to assist others in developing a vivid relationship with God. When a ministry begins to resemble the ministry of Jesus, the next step is to teach and mentor others to do the same. This need has been the passion and motivation behind the call on Jim's life.

In 1991, Jim founded Jim Hockaday Ministries, Inc. Through the years, he has traveled and ministered in churches both in the United States and abroad. He has also been privileged to travel to and minister in several Rhema Bible Training Centers around the world.

Jim resides in the Tulsa area with his wife Erin (a 1991 graduate of Rhema Bible Training Center and a former member of The Rhema Singers and Band for two and a half years), and their young daughters Alli, Drew, and Chloe.

Books Published

Qualified For A Miracle
Secrets to Receiving From God
ISBN 1-57794-213-2
Copyright © 2002 by Jim Hockaday
P.O. Box 839
Broken Arrow, Oklahoma 74013

Published by **Harrison House, Inc.**
P.O. Box 35035
Tulsa, Oklahoma 74153
Date of 1st Printing: June 2002
Printed in the United States of America

Until I Come
The Works I Do You Shall Do Also
ISBN 1-893301-05-2
Copyright © 2002 by Jim Hockaday
P.O. Box 839
Broken Arrow, Oklahoma 74013

Published by Jim Hockaday Ministries, Inc.
P.O. Box 839
Broken Arrow, Oklahoma 74013
Date of 1st Printing: September 2002
Date of 2nd Printing: June 2003
Printed in the United States of America

Living In The Miraculous
Guaranteed!
ISBN 1-893301-12-5 (pbk.)

P.O. Box 839
Broken Arrow, Oklahoma 74013

Published by Jim Hockaday Ministries, Inc.
P.O. Box 839
Broken Arrow, Oklahoma
Date of 1st Printing: June 2003
Printed in the United States of America

CONTACT IMFORMATION

To contact the Author please write:

Jim Hockaday Ministries, Inc.
P.O. Box 839
Broken Arrow, OK 74013

You can also visit us on the web at:
(E-Mail access only through the Web)
www.jimhockadaymin.com

We welcome your comments, prayer requests, and especially your miracles!

www.jimhockadaymin.com

www.jimhockadaymin.com